Do You Know What Day Tomorrow Is?

A TEACHER'S ALMANAC

By Lee Bennett Hopkins
and Misha Arenstein

CITATION PRESS   NEW YORK   1975

FOR REPRINT PERMISSION, GRATEFUL ACKNOWLEDGMENT IS MADE TO:

Atheneum Publishers for "August" by Myra Cohn Livingston from THE MALIBU AND OTHER POEMS (A Margaret K. McElderry Book), copyright © 1972 by Myra Cohn Livingston, and "Landscape" by Eve Merriam from FINDING A POEM, copyright © 1970 by Eve Merriam.

Thomas Y. Crowell Company, Inc. for "Labor Day" by Aileen Fisher from SKIP AROUND THE YEAR, copyright © 1967 by Aileen Fisher.

Harper & Row, Publishers, Inc. for "Rudolph Is Tired of the City" by Gwendolyn Brooks from BRONZEVILLE BOYS AND GIRLS, copyright © 1956 by Gwendolyn Brooks Blakely.

Holt, Rinehart and Winston, Inc. for "The Pasture" by Robert Frost from THE POETRY OF ROBERT FROST edited by Edward Connery Lathem, copyright, © 1939, 1967 1969 by Holt, Rinehart and Winston, Inc.

Alfred A. Knopf, Inc. for "Dreams" by Langston Hughes from DON'T YOU TURN BACK, copyright © 1932 by Alfred A. Knopf, Inc. and renewed 1960 by Langston Hughes.

Published by Citation Press, Library and Trade Division, Scholastic Magazines, Inc.
Editorial Office: 50 West 44th Street, New York, New York 10036.

Library of Congress Catalog Card Number: 75-23145

International Standard Book Numbers:
0-590-07444-X (Hardcover)
0-590-09604-4 (Paperback)

Printed in the U.S.A.

Jacket design by Constance Ftera

1   2   3   4   5   79   78   77   76   75

To Selma Rich Brody

whose days are filled

with apricot tomorrows

L.B.H.

M.A.

CONTENTS

JNTRODUCTJON

Do You Know What Day Tomorrow Is? is a compendium
of concise information about people, places, events, and
fun-facts especially selected to tie in with every area of the
elementary school curriculum. The text grew out of actual
experiences we have enjoyed sharing with children and
many that children have developed with us. Girls and boys
eagerly celebrate happenings; in the process they gain insight into historical and contemporary affairs and develop
appreciation of people and events.

We firmly believe that children are more responsive when
they are called upon to participate in a plan, and, there-
fore, numerous opportunities are suggested for involving
students with the book's content. You and your students can
use the almanac as a constant reminder of what's coming
or what's here.

Each month contains information on birthdays of famous
people from a variety of professions and cultures—historical
personages, scientists, artists, musicians, writers, religious
leaders, and sports personalities. All the major holidays
and some minor ones are described—how they came to be
celebrated and how they are observed in various places
both in America and around the world today. To round
out the year, we have included unusual events and interest-

[xi]

ing facts about taken-for-granted things that children will enjoy learning about. Each chapter begins with a brief account of the origin of the month's name as well as a poem of the month—poetry selected from both the past and the contemporary scene.

Many a day can be enlivened when children celebrate something; youngsters delight in real ceremonies, especially when they help bring joy into classrooms. Students in the middle- and upper-grades can use the book on their own for preplanning things to come. It is hoped that the entries will encourage them to supplement the facts presented by flavoring them with their own additional findings.

A rotating group of students can serve as a calendar committee, scouring the almanac for facts to share with classmates. If possible, children can produce daily or weekly *You-Are-There*-type broadcasts over the school's public address system in which they highlight events and share information with the entire school.

Another technique is to encourage a group of students to become current event historians; they can add contemporary dates and events to the volume's daily records.

All the reference books and nonprint media cited have been carefully reviewed and chosen with children in mind; they provide many opportunities for multilevel reading and learning about the same event. School or public librarians can direct children to these sources, most of which are works by popular writers for children.

This volume was planned to dip in and dip out of. Use it when you can and when you want to, weekly, monthly, or every day. Individual entries contain practical, tried-and-tested ideas for activities that children can and have engaged in.

We hope these accounts of people and events will prompt

students to want to learn more and to explore the subjects further in the wide world of books and nonprint media.

Happy reading, happy teaching, and happy every day!

Lee Bennett Hopkins
Misha Arenstein
Scarborough, New York
April 1975

SEPTEMBER

Flower—Aster   Birthstone—Sapphire

The name September comes from the Latin word *septem* meaning *seven*. Originally September was the seventh month in the Roman calendar.

POEM OF THE MONTH

LABOR DAY

Today the mills are silent,
the foundaries make no sound . . .
today we honor those who work
to make the wheels go round.

The looms, the lathes, the hammers,
the great machines are stilled . . .
today we honor those who weave,
and mine, and weld, and build.

Our soldiers have their medals,
our statesmen have their praise . . .
today we honor those who work
in scores of other ways.

—Aileen Fisher

SEPTEMBER 1, 1939
World War II Began

German troops crossed the Polish frontier launching the beginning of a six-year war that killed almost forty million people. Adolf Hitler, the Nazi dictator, succeeded in seizing most of Europe almost effortlessly as the forces allied against him—the British Commonwealth, France, and the U.S.S.R.—reeled under the new type of war the Germans had invented. The *blitzkrieg*, or lightning war, of 1940 introduced air bombings that destroyed major cities, massive tank attacks that crushed ill-equipped armies in France, Scandinavia, and the Balkans, and the ruthless suppression of civilian populations.

On December 7, 1941, the Japanese attack on Pearl

Harbor brought the United States into the war on the side of Britian and Russia. Opposing the Allies were the Axis Powers of Japan, Italy, and Germany. After almost six long years of widespread conflict, the Allies were victorious on all fronts in 1945.

There are scores of books for children about this period of history. A display of these volumes can help children understand the horrors of war for both soldiers and civilians.

SEPTEMBER 1, 1974

A United States Air Force spy plane, a SR-71 reconnaissance jet, broke the speed record between New York and London. It flew at approximately three times the speed of sound and made the 3,490 mile transatlantic crossing in one hour, fifty-five minutes, and forty-two seconds. Its average speed was 1,817 miles an hour. The previous record of four hours and forty-six minutes was set in 1969 by a British royal phantom fighter.

SEPTEMBER 5, 1847
Birth Date of Jesse Woodson James

Jesse James, an American outlaw and legendary figure, was born at Centerville, now Kearney, Clay County, Missouri. At the outbreak of the Civil War the James family favored the South. Jesse and his brother Frank joined the guerilla band led by William Clarke Quantrill and served with it until the end of the war. In 1866 enemies declared Jesse an outlaw. For the next sixteen years he carried out a campaign of banditry that made him famous—the American equivalent of Robin Hood. In Iowa in 1873, James, along with a group of confederates, staged a new kind of highway robbery when they held up their first train. Nine years later he moved to St. Joseph, Missouri, changed his name to Tom Howard, and posed as a cattle buyer. In the later part of this year he was shot in the head by Robert Ford, a member of the band who had turned traitor.

SEPTEMBER 6, 1620

The Pilgrims sailed on the *Mayflower* from Plymouth, England, to settle in the New World. An account of what the voyage was like is given in *If You Sailed on the Mayflower* by Ann McGovern (Four Winds Press, 1970; Scholastic Book Services, paper).

LABOR DAY
The First Monday in September

This legal holiday is observed on the first Monday in September to honor American workers. In 1886 the American Federation of Labor, one of America's earliest and largest unions, proclaimed that "it shall be as uncommon for a man to work on that day as on Independence Day." The nation's first Labor Day parade was held on September 5, 1882, in New York City, although the holiday was not made a national one until 1894 when President Grover Cleveland signed a bill making it a legal holiday. The founder of Labor Day was Peter J. Maguire, a carpenter and founder of the United Brotherhood of Carpenters and Joiners. Each Labor Day memorial services are held at Mr. Maguire's grave in Philadelphia, Pennsylvania. *Labor Day* by James Marnell, (T. Y. Crowell, 1966) is an easy-to-read text that tells the history of the holiday.

SEPTEMBER 7, 1860
Birth Date of Anna Mary Robertson Moses

Ms. Moses, better known as Grandma Moses, began to paint in 1938 at age seventy-eight. She was one of ten children born on a farm in Washington County, New York. Her education was limited for, in her own words, "Little girls did not go to school much in winter owing to the cold and not enough clothing." Her feeling for art showed itself when she was quite young, but she was discouraged by her mother.

After the death of her husband in 1927, Grandma Moses began to embroider to fill empty hours. When her hands became too crippled from arthritis to hold a needle, she turned to oil painting. Her first oil was done on thresher cloth with some old paints she found in the barn on her farm. Later she ordered paint and some brushes from a mail order house and began to copy postcard scenes and Currier and Ives prints. She soon turned to painting scenes representing experiences from her own life. In 1939 her work was discovered, and in 1940 her first one-woman show was held in New York City. Since then her work, described as "authentic American primitive," has become an American legend.

Younger children can read further about the life of Grandma Moses in *Grandma Moses: Favorite Painter* by Charles P. Graves (Garrard, 1969); more mature readers will enjoy *Barefoot in the Grass: The Story of Grandma Moses* (Doubleday, 1970), by William H. Armstrong, winner of the 1970 Newbery Medal for *Sounder* (Harper, 1969). His book contains ten full-color paintings by the artist.

[5]

SEPTEMBER 9, 1757
Birth Date of Marquis de Lafayette

By the time French-born Lafayette reached the age of thirty, he had made himself one of the world's foremost fighters for freedom. He served in George Washington's army as a major general, suffered the hardships of Valley Forge (1777–1778), and supported his fellow Frenchmen's desires for justice and equality after Americans won their fight for independence.

SEPTEMBER 9, 1850

California became the thirty-first state.

SEPTEMBER 9, 1906
Birth Date of Aileen Fisher

Aileen Fisher grew up around the little town of Iron River on the Upper Peninsula of Michigan, near the Wisconsin border. Currently she lives in Boulder, Colorado, where she enjoys woodworking, hiking, mountain climbing, and all forms of nature.

Since Ms. Fisher has written poetry for all age levels, why not celebrate her birthday by reading the class one of her poems? You or your students will find many books by her in almost any school or public library. *Skip Around the Year* (T. Y. Crowell, 1967) is a joyous calendar of holiday verses. Besides the September poem of the month, "Labor Day," you will find such poems as "For the UN on Its Birthday," "Voting Machine," and "Light the Festive Candles (for Hanukkah)." Other popular titles by the poet include *In the Middle of the Night* (1965), *Sing Little Mouse* (1969), *Clean As a Whistle* (1969), *In One Door and*

[6]

Out the Other (1970), and *Feathered Ones and Furry* (1971; all published by T. Y. Crowell). Ms. Fisher can be heard reading thirty-one of her poems on the recording *Poetry Parade* (Weston Woods).

SEPTEMBER 10, 1846

Elias Howe patented the sewing machine. His apprenticeship as a machinist and cotton mill worker helped him develop a machine that revolutionized the sewing industry. His invention took five years to perfect. He sold his patent for $1,250 in England because little interest was shown in it in the United States. Later American manufacturers tried using his invention free; he sued for royalties and won the case.

SEPTEMBER 13, 1895

The first professional game of football was played at Latrobe, Pennsylvania, between the local YMCA team and the Jeannette (Pennsylvania) Athletic Club. Each player received $10. The game, played by two teams of eleven players each on a rectangular field, apparently began in ancient Greece and Rome. It was brought to America as early as the seventeenth century. Football has come a long way. Today the professional game is a complex, highly profitable operation. Joe Namath, the well-known quarterback for the New York Jets, for example, earns a higher salary than the president of the United States.

Interested students might research the history of football from ancient times to the present and prepare a time line of "Great Events and Great Players in Football."

SEPTEMBER 14, 1814

> Oh, say, can you see by the dawn's early light,
> What so proudly we hail'd at the twilight's
> last gleaming . . .

Francis Scott Key, a Baltimore attorney, wrote the words to "The Star-Spangled Banner" in a Baltimore hotel room after witnessing the British bombardment of Fort McHenry from a ship in Chesapeake Bay. Key gave the manuscript to his brother-in-law, J. H. Nicholson, the next day. The manuscript remained in the Nicholson family for almost one hundred years. In 1953 the Maryland Historical Society bought it for $26,400. Key made three additional copies of the poem; one is owned by the Pennsylvania Historical Society, another by the Library of Congress, and the third has disappeared. The words were sung to the tune of an old English tavern refrain, "To Anacreon in Heaven." It was sung for the first time in Baltimore.

On March 3, 1931, President Herbert Hoover signed a bill making "The Star-Spangled Banner" the national anthem. Today the flag that inspired the song is displayed in the Museum of History and Technology in Washington, D. C.

The Story of the Star-Spangled Banner (Doubleday, 1973) is joyously and gloriously illustrated by Peter Spier. Music is provided at the back of the book and includes guitar chords. The volume also contains a historical note about the song and a reproduction of Key's original manuscript. Endpapers depict full-color reproductions of "A Collection of Flags of the American Revolution and Those of the United States of America, Its Government, and Armed Forces."

SEPTEMBER 15, 1857
Birth Date of William Howard Taft

Twenty-seventh President

    Born in: Cincinnati, Ohio
    Occupation: Lawyer, professor, judge
    President: 1909–1913, Republican
    Died: March 8, 1930
                 Washington, D.C.
                 Buried in Arlington, Virginia

About Taft

▩ Only president to serve as chief justice of the Supreme Court after his term of office.

▩ First governor general of the Philippines.

During His Term

▩ Continued Theodore Roosevelt's anti-trust and conservation policies.

▩ Started custom of president throwing out baseball to start each season.

SEPTEMBER 16, 1810
Mexico's Independence Day

In 1519 Hernando Cortes led a small army of conquistadores, or conquerors, from the east coast of Mexico to its capital in the interior. They soon crushed the Aztec Empire and its legendary leader Montezuma. This set the stage for three hundred years of autocratic rule of Mexico by Spain. The first serious challenge to Spanish domination was made on this date by Miguel Hidalgo, a village priest of Indian background. He issued his "Grito of Dolores," calling upon all Mexicans to revolt against the pure-blooded Spaniards who had oppressed them for three centuries. Although Hidalgo's crusade attracted thousands of armed supporters who liberated many major towns and cities, it failed. The priest was executed in 1811, and Mexico endured ten more years of Spanish rule.

Annually Mexico's president reenacts Hidalgo's heroic act, "Grito" is read, and the Independence Day bell rung by the priest is rung again. Mexicans thus honor the call for freedom issued by the simple priest from the Parish of Dolores.

SEPTEMBER 17–23
Constitution Week

This week celebrates the anniversary of the signing of the Constitution of the United States on September 17, 1787. This document, the world's oldest written laws of government, was drawn up by members of the Constitutional Convention who met in Philadelphia. The Constitution went into effect nine months later, June 21, 1788, when it was ratified by nine states and replaced the Articles of Conferation. The Constitution spells out the responsibilities of the three branches of the federal government —the executive, legislative, and judicial—and how they check and balance each other. It also defines the relations of the states to the federal government and sets forth the amendment process by which the Constitution can be changed, added to, and brought up to date. Twenty-six such changes have been made since the Constitution was adopted. Because it can be altered, people feel the Constitution will never become too old-fashioned or rigid. What do your students think about this?

Your class might prepare a time line showing when the fifty states entered the Union. (All this information in given within this book.) Traced outlines of the individual states can be transferred to colored construction paper, cut out, and placed in chronological order to depict the growth of the United States.

SEPTEMBER 19, 1928

Mickey Mouse, the lovable character created by Walt Disney, first appeared in a movie cartoon. Mickey became immensely popular and introduced a new trend in the motion picture industry—animated cartoons. Ask how many children in your class have visited a Disneyland, and discuss their experiences.

SEPTEMBER 20, 1519

Ferdinand Magellan, a Portuguese nobleman, set forth on his epic three-year voyage around the world. Dissatisfied with his treatment by the Portuguese king, Magellan had sought support from neighboring Spain. Flying the Spanish flag, his five ships and two hundred and seventy seamen sailed west to reach the Eastern Spice Islands. In the process they dramatically demonstrated a fact we routinely accept today—the earth is round! The voyage entailed finding a passage around the tip of South America (today's Strait of Magellan), entering a new ocean (the Pacific, which he named), and exploring new lands, among them the Philippines where Magellan was murdered. Only one of his ships completed the voyage; it returned to Spain in September 1522.

Children can trace Magellan's voyage on a world map; this will impress upon them the length and hardship of such a journey. Perhaps they can use airline tables to compare its duration with jet travel today.

SEPTEMBER 21
Beginning of Autumn

Because the earth is tilted on its axis as it moves around the sun, different amounts of light and heat fall on different areas of our planet during the year, causing spring, summer, autumn, and winter. The arrival of new seasons is most marked in temperate regions, where the sun rises highest in the sky during summer and lowest in winter. Scientists have set approximate dates for the arrival of each of the four seasons in the Northern Hemisphere: autumn, September 21; winter, December 21; spring, March 21; and summer, June 21. The summer and winter dates are called solstices and mark the days of longest and shortest daylight. Spring and autumn occur when the sun is directly over the equator; these times are called equinoxes.

Mark the arrival of each season by taking the class on a short neighborhood field trip. Let students look for the first signs of the season and perhaps collect some materials for a science table display. Several children can visit the school or public library to seek books about the particular season. These can be added to the display. Time might also be set aside for some brainstorming in which the children list words to describe the coming season. The words can be copied and/or mimeographed for each child to have to use in creative expression exercises.

Older children will enjoy *Fall Is Here* by Dorothy Sterling (Doubleday, 1966), which describes simply and accurately the changes that take place in nature. The text is accompanied by illustrations in black and white and color.

SEPTEMBER 21, 1959

Hawaii became the fiftieth state.

SEPTEMBER 23, 480 B.C.
Birth Date of Euripides

Euripides was the last of the three most famous Greek dramatists of the ancient world. The first was Aeschylus, the second Sophocles. It is said that Euripides was born on this day—the day the Greeks defeated the Persians in the great sea battle of Salamis. The plays of Euripides are still widely read and performed throughout the world.

Older boys and girls can read and/or perform four adaptations of his plays using Albert Cullum's *Greek Tears and Roman Laughter* (Citation Press, 1970). The plays include "Iphigenia in Aulus," "The Trojan Women," "Alcestis," and "Hecuba." An introduction to each play gives background information and ideas for presentation as well as a vocabulary list and a cast of characters. The volume also includes two plays by Sophocles and four by Aeschylus.

SEPTEMBER 23, 1838
Birth Date of Victoria Claflin Woodhull

Did a woman ever run for president of the United States? Yes, indeed! Victoria Claflin Woodhull attempted this in 1872. She was an unconventional reformer who fought for women's rights. In later years she became an early patron of aviation and offered a prize of $5,000 in 1914 for the first transatlantic flight.

Perhaps a group of students would like to nominate other women for president—either from the past or from among those who are active currently.

SEPTEMBER 23, 1846

The planet Neptune was accidentally discovered because of its neighbor Uranus' strange behavior—it failed to

reappear where mathematicians and astronomers calculated its orbit would take it. Scientists were very puzzled
and remained so for twenty years. This mystery was solved
with the discovery of Neptune by two German astronomers.
This large solar body's gravitational pull accounted for
Uranus' erratic orbit. Neptune, a greenish mass, is the
eighth most distant planet from the sun. It has two
satellites (Triton and Nereid) and takes about 165 years to
revolve once around the sun.

SEPTEMBER 24

The zodiac sign, Libra the Scales, begins today and ends
on October 23. How many children in the class were born
under this sign?

SEPTEMBER 24, 1898
Birth Date of Harry Behn

> When children ask me how I write a poem, I
> have to say I don't know. When they ask me to
> *tell* them how to write a poem, I dare, timidly,
> to suggest something like this: "Learn to love
> words, to know how they look, what they mean,
> how they sound."*

It wasn't until Harry Behn was fifty years old that he
began writing poetry for children. At that time he moved
to Connecticut to devote his life to writing and travel.
Why not celebrate his birthday by sharing one of his
poems? With younger children you might read *The Little*

---

* Harry Behn. *Chrysalis: Concerning Children and Poetry*. New York:
Harcourt, 1968, p. 19.

Hill (1949), *All Kinds of Time* (1950), or *Windy Morning* (1953). Older children will enjoy *The Golden Hive* (1966) or one of his widely acclaimed translations of Japanese haiku, *Cricket Songs* (1964) or *More Cricket Songs* (1971; all published by Harcourt). Sharing selections from these books might spark budding poets in your classroom. Teachers can read Mr. Behn's views on poetry in *Chrysalis: Concerning Children and Poetry* (Harcourt, 1968); he can be heard reading his work for children on the recording *Poetry Parade* (Weston Woods).

SEPTEMBER 25, 1513

Vasco Nuñez de Balboa, a Spanish conqueror and explorer, became the first European to see the eastern shore of the Pacific Ocean. Four days later he waded into the ocean and claimed it and all its shores for Spain. His discovery paved the way for the Spanish exploration and conquest of the western coast of South America. The Spanish called the ocean the South Sea because it lay south of the Isthmus of Panama, a strip of land connecting North and South America. Later in 1520 Ferdinand Magellan sailed across the ocean and found its waters quiet and calm. He named it the Pacific meaning *peaceful*.

SEPTEMBER 26, 1774
Birth Date of Johnny "Appleseed" Chapman

Johnny Appleseed was an American frontier nurseryman who became a major folk hero because of his interest in growing apple trees. He is considered the first planter of orchards all across America. He died in March 1845, near Fort Wayne, Indiana, where a city park and other monuments honor his unmarked grave.

Share a poem or story about John Chapman with the class—while all munch on an apple, of course! Children who want to know more about this legendary figure can read *The Story of Johnny Appleseed*, written and illustrated by Aliki (Prentice-Hall, 1963) or *Johnny Appleseed* by Eva Moore (Scholastic Book Services, paper).

SEPTEMBER 27, 1822
Birth Date of Hiram Rhodes Revels

Hiram Rhodes Revels was born free in Fayetteville, North Carolina. On February 25, 1870, he took office as a United States senator, the first black to achieve this position. He represented Mississippi, the state he adopted after the Civil War, until March 3, 1871. A great deal of his life was devoted to church work. He was an ordained minister in the African Methodist Church and organized many black churches.

SEPTEMBER 30, 1966

Bechuanaland, today called Botswana, a region of Southern Africa, achieved independence from Britain. Botswana contains the Kalahari Desert, an area inhabited by the Bushmen; these primitive people survive in a harsh environment, testifying to man's amazing ability to adapt to hostile places.

END OF SEPTEMBER
American Indian Day

American Indian Day, usually celebrated on the last Friday in September, honors native Americans. This is an excellent time to discuss the plight of the American

Indian, past and present. Some resource materials include: *Historical American Indian Biographies* and *Contemporary American Indian Biographies,* available from Instructor Publications, are two kits containing thirty-two large-sized study prints. Forty-eight-page teacher's guides contain biographies of each of the individuals portrayed on the prints, along with follow-up activities to encourage students to investigate Indian culture and life styles. Personalities include American Indians from many tribes and professions to show the diversity of Indian culture.

For younger readers suggest *The Trees Stand Shining: Poetry of North American Indians* selected by Hettie Jones (Dial, 1971). Eleven biographies of Indian men and woman are available from Garrard Publishers. Included among them and written on a third-grade reading level are: *Black Hawk: Indian Patriot* by LaVere Anderson (1972), *Pocahontas: Indian Princess* by Katherine E. Wilkie (1969), and *Massasoit: Friend of the Pilgrims* by Virginia Voight (1971). All titles have been checked for accuracy by anthropologists Alice Marriott and Carol K. Rachlin.

For older readers suggest: *In the Trail of the Wind: American Indian Poems and Ritual Orations* by John Bierhorst (Farrar, Straus, 1971), *The Defenders: Osceola, Techumseh, Cochise* by Ann McGovern. (Scholastic Book Services, 1970; also in paper), and *The False Treaty: The Removal of the Cherokees from Georgia* by Anne Terry White (Scholastic Book Services, 1970; also in paper).

A good teacher reference is *The Real Americans* by Hyatt A. Verrell (Putnam, 1963). A free, sixty-four-page bibliography is available from the Association on American Indian Affairs; *Preliminary Bibliography of Selected Children's Books About American Indians* is a listing of carefully selected books that portray the American Indian honestly.

SEPTEMBER/OCTOBER
Jewish Holidays

Jewish holidays have been celebrated for over five thousand years. Two important Jewish holidays, Rosh Hashanah and Yom Kippur, fall during the months of September or October. (Be sure to check your school calendar to find out the exact dates this year.)

The blowing of the shofar, the hollow horn of a male sheep, calls Jews to gather in their synagogues to mark Rosh Hashanah, the beginning of a new year. This holiday commences with the start of the seventh Hebrew month, Tishri—September or October of today's calendar. Traditionally God was asked to provide rainfall for crops, spare those who committed minor sins, and grant a new year of happiness. Believers have ten days, until Yom Kippur, to seek forgiveness. God opens the "Book of Life" on this holiday, reads all deeds and thoughts of his followers, and determines their fate for the coming year.

Annually ancient Hebrews selected a goat to send into the wilderness; this specially selected creature was thought to carry the sins of the community away with it. Today Yom Kippur celebrates this ritual of ancient times. It is the Day of Atonement for all Hebrews—a twenty-four-hour period of fasting and asking God to forgive the personal and general sins of man. Translated, Yom means *day*, and Kippur, *cleansing from sin*. Believers gather in synagogues to seek guidance from their religious leader, the rabbi. All commit themselves to living according to the rules of the Torah (Bible). Yom Kippur is observed ten days after Rosh Hashanah.

Girls and boys can learn more about these two holidays plus other Jewish celebrations in two easy-to-read informative books, *Jewish Holidays* by Betty Morrow and Louis Hartman (Garrard, 1967) and *The Jewish New Year* by Molly Cone (T. Y. Crowell, 1966).

OCTOBER

Flower—Marigold   Birthstone—Opal

October comes from the Latin word *octo* meaning *eighth*.
October was the eighth month in the Roman calendar.

POEM OF THE MONTH

THREE GHOSTESSES

Three little ghostesses,
Sitting on postesses,
Eating buttered toastesses,
Greasing their fistesses,
Up to their wristesses,
Oh, what beastesses
To make such feastesses!

—Anonymous

FIRE PREVENTION WEEK

Usually during the early part of October, one week is designated Fire Prevention Week. Statistics show that awareness of fire prevention techniques is important. There are approximately two and a half million home fires yearly in the United States that cause billions of dollars worth of damage and loss of life. Forest fires are another area of great concern. During 1971, 90 percent of the fires reported were caused by man; 10 percent were caused by lightning.

Discuss the positive and negative uses of fire with the class and ways they can help prevent fires. A walk around the school and community can be planned to look at fire hydrants, extinguishers, alarm boxes, fire exits, and, where possible, the location of the nearest firehouse. Younger children can learn a great deal from a visit to the local fire station; for upper grades fire fighters can be invited to speak to the class on fire prevention practices and the duties they perform. Children in the lower grades might also write a group letter to Smokey the Bear, asking specific questions about fire and/or fire prevention. The address is:

Smokey the Bear, United States Forest Service, Department of Agriculture, Washington, D. C. 20252. The children's letters will be answered. All children can create fire prevention posters to display around the classroom, school, or community.

OCTOBER 2, 1800
Birth Date of Nat Turner

One of the major slave revolts of nineteenth century America was led by Nat Turner, a slave-preacher in Virginia. He declared God had told him to lead his people out of bondage. On Sunday, August 21, 1831, Turner, four disciples, and two other slaves attacked and killed Turner's master and his entire family. The group then attracted more slaves. All that night and the following day they went from plantation to plantation, freeing slaves and slaying whites in an abortive attempt to lead a liberation movement of Southern slaves. When the rebellion was suppressed, Turner went into hiding for two months. He was finally captured and hanged in Jerusalem, Virginia, along with the other participants in this uprising. Nat Turner's revolt is early evidence of black people's determination to win freedom at any cost.

Violence is a subject that is often in the news—whether for a just or unjust purpose. Older children will find the topic one of concern, one that will spark much debate. The story of Nat Turner can serve as a jumping-off point for one or a series of classroom panel discussions.

OCTOBER 2, 1869
Birth Date of Mohandas Karamchand Gandhi

Gandhi, an intensely religious man, opposed any form of violence. The Indian people looked upon him as a saint and called him *mahatma,* meaning *great soul.* Gandhi was instrumental in gaining India's independence from the British. He urged his followers to boycott anything English. His nonviolent resistance tactics served as models for nonviolent social change in many parts of the world, and his philosophy inspired the late Dr. Martin Luther King, Jr.

Gandhi was the son of an Indian merchant. He studied law in England and in 1893 went to South Africa where he first encountered racial discrimination. In 1915 he returned to India and five years later became a leader of India's Congress Party, a political organization working for independence. After one of his campaigns against British rule, he was jailed. In fact, he spent many years of his life in prison for his beliefs.

In 1934 Gandhi resigned from the Congress Party to devote his full time to encouraging village industries, hoping that this would make India economically independent of the British. Britain finally granted independence to India in 1947. The following year Gandhi was assassinated by a fanatical Hindu youth.

OCTOBER 4, 1181 OR 1182
Birth Date of St. Francis of Assisi

Each year the feast of St. Francis is celebrated in memory of St. Francis of Assisi. St. Francis was the son of a wealthy merchant. When he was twenty he fought for his native Assisi in a battle with the neighboring city of Perugia. Assisi lost, Francis was captured and imprisoned for a year. When he returned home, he became gravely ill and began to devote his life to prayer and service to the poor. He and his many followers formed the Franciscan Order of Monks, which is devoted to poverty and prayer. The hilltop town of Assisi in central Italy where St. Francis was born and died is visited by travelers from throughout the world each year. Today the Franciscan Order and the separate order for women, the Poor Clares, are still widely known for their charity, education, and missionary work.

OCTOBER 4, 1822
Birth Date of Rutherford B. Hayes

Nineteenth President
>   Born in: Delaware, Ohio
>   Occupation: Lawyer
>   President: 1877–1881, Republican
>   Died: January 17, 1893
>   Fremont, Ohio

About Hayes
- Unpaid defense attorney for fugitive slaves.
- Civil War general.
- Governor of Ohio for three terms.
- Became president in disputed election against Samuel J. Tilden. Neither received an electoral majority until three days before Inauguration Day as an electoral commission investigated the voting returns in three Southern states.

During His Term
- Ended Reconstruction period by taking troops out of the South.
- His wife, Lucy, started the custom of rolling Easter eggs on the White House lawn.

OCTOBER 4, 1957

A device the size of a basketball was rocketed into orbit around the earth by the Soviet Union. *Sputnik I*, meaning *fellow-traveler*, was the first man-made satellite. Its 184 pounds completed a trip around the earth every ninety-six minutes. This set the stage for later manned flights by Russian and American astronauts.

OCTOBER 5, 1830
Birth Date of Chester A. Arthur

Twenty-first President

Born in:	Fairfield, Vermont
Occupation:	Lawyer
President:	1881–1885
Died:	November 18, 1886
	New York, New York

About Arthur

▨ Elected vice-president and became president when James A. Garfield died, seven months after being shot by an assassin.

During His Term

▨ Fought for establishment of the Civil Service Commission to end the era of widespread corruption and patronage in federal jobs.

▨ Most elegantly dressed president since Washington.

▨ Refurnished the White House in Victorian splendor.

OCTOBER 9
Leif Ericson Day

Leif Ericson Day was proclaimed in 1964. Ericson, a Norse adventurer, was nicknamed Leif the Lucky. Around the year 1000, he unintentionally discovered North America while attempting to sail to Greenland from Norway. He called his discovery Vinland, and historians think he landed at Labrador or Newfoundland. Recently he has been given credit for being one of several individuals who touched upon the North American continent before Christopher Columbus.

Today is a good time for a group of students to trace Ericson's route on a world map. Students might compare his voyage with that of Columbus (see October 12). The subject of great things people find by accident might spark a good discussion among middle-grade students.

OCTOBER 9, 1915

The International Association for Criminal Identification, or the Fingerprint Society, was formed in Oakland, California. It is believed that the Chinese used thumbprints to sign documents long before the birth of Christ. In 1858, Sir William Herschel developed a method of identifying fingerprints.

Plan a bulletin board display of "Our Thumbprints." Each child in the class can print his or her thumbprints on a piece of paper using paint or ink—washable, of course! Let the children compare the prints to see how each is different.

OCTOBER 10, 1973

Vice-president Spiro T. Agnew, serving under President Richard M. Nixon, resigned from his office, the second vice-president in the country's history to resign. The first was John C. Calhoun, the famed Southern orator who stepped down from his office on December 28, 1832, after a political feud with President Andrew Jackson over the issue of states' rights.

Many vice-presidents in American history have interesting pasts. You can read about them in *The Vice-Presidents* of the United States by John D. and Emalie P. Feerick (Watts, 1969; also in paper). The volume contains information on the office, brief biographies, and photographs and engravings of the vice-presidents.

OCTOBER 11, 1884
Birth Date of Eleanor Roosevelt

As America's most famous First Lady from 1933 to 1945, Eleanor, wife of President Franklin Delano Roosevelt, became a legend in her own time. She was not content to merely be the White House hostess. She spent a great deal of time being the "legs and eyes" for her husband who was crippled with polio. She traveled extensively, investigating many types of institutions and localities during the Depression, and during World War II she acted as an ambassador of goodwill to other countries and visited military camps abroad. After her husband's death, President Truman appointed her United States delegate to the United Nations. Her major accomplishments were with the Commission on Human Rights where she worked on problems of resettling refugees of World War II.

Several fine biographies about this incredible woman are available for children. For younger readers there is *Eleanor Roosevelt* by Jane Goodsell (T. Y. Crowell, 1970; also in paper); upper graders might enjoy *The Story of Eleanor Roosevelt* by Margaret Davidson (Four Winds Press, 1969; also in paper, from Scholastic Book Services) and *The Story of Eleanor Roosevelt* by Jeanette Eaton (Morrow, 1956).

OCTOBER 12, 1492

Christopher Columbus sighted San Salvador in Central America. Today Columbus is honored on the second Monday of October. Since most students are somewhat familiar with the circumstances surrounding this explorer's feat— the discovery of the islands in the Caribbean Sea—have a group locate the exact place Columbus found on this date. Additional research can focus on recent theories regarding other earlier explorers of the New World.

There are many biographies of Columbus. Younger readers will enjoy *Christopher Columbus* by Ann McGovern (Scholastic Book Services, paper). For older readers there are *Columbus and the New World* by August Derleth (Farrar, Straus, 1957) and *Admiral Christopher Columbus* by Clara Ingram Judson (Follett, 1965). An easy-to-read account of the holiday itself appears in *Columbus Day* by Paul Showers (T. Y. Crowell, 1965).

OCTOBER 13, 1754?
Birth Date of Mary Ludwig Hays McCauley

Ms. McCauley, better known as Molly Pitcher, was a Pennsylvania-born heroine of the War for American Independence. She joined her husband, John Hays, at Valley Forge, where both endured the harsh conditions forced upon the Continental army. On June 28, 1778, at the Battle of Monmouth, she was given the name Molly Pitcher by Washington's soldiers because of her ceaseless work providing water to the exhausted troops. In this same fight she manned her husband's cannon after he was wounded and continued firing the weapon until the battle was over.

OCTOBER 14, 1644
Birth Date of William Penn

One might wonder why the son of a famous English admiral would endure prison, ostracism, and poverty for his religious beliefs. William Penn, founder of the Pennsylvania Colony, pursued this course when he became a Quaker in his native Britain. In 1682, when Penn's father died, King Charles II gave young Penn title to an enormous area of land in the American colonies to wipe out a royal debt to the elder Penn. Penn named the area *Sylvania*, meaning *woods*, because of its immense forests. Pennsylvania became a refuge for thousands of Europeans seeking religious freedom; even Indians were fairly treated in this Quaker dominated state.

Three easy-to-read books that tell about the life of William Penn are: *The Story of William Penn* by Aliki (Prentice-Hall, 1964), *William Penn: American Pioneer* by Betty Ellen Haughey (Putnam, 1968), and *William Penn: Friend to All* by Katherine E. Wilkie (Garrard, 1954).

OCTOBER 14, 1890
Birth Date of Dwight David Eisenhower

Thirty-fourth President

Born in:	Denison, Texas
Occupation:	Soldier
President:	1953–1961, Republican
Died:	March 28, 1969
	Washington, D.C.
	Buried in Abilene, Kansas

About Eisenhower

- Came from a poor family.
- West Point education led to an army career.
- Supreme Commander of Allied forces in Europe during World War II.
- President of Columbia University.
- Chose Richard M. Nixon as his vice-president.

During His Terms

🏴 Ended Korean War.

🏴 Started space program when Russians launched first satellite, *Sputnik I.*

🏴 Historic Supreme Court decision against segregation in public schools on May 17, 1954.

OCTOBER 16, 1758
Birth Date of Noah Webster

In 1828 Noah Webster published his *American Diction-ary of the English Language,* a job that had taken him fifty years to complete. New editions of Webster's diction-ary are still issued periodically. Celebrate Mr. Webster's birth date by having each child in the class look through a dictionary to find a new word she or he particularly likes and can use.

OCTOBER 20, 1891
Birth Date of Sir James Chadwick

Sir James Chadwick spent much of his life doing re-search on radioactivity. He discovered an unknown part of the atomic building block of all matter—the neutron—in 1932 and later demonstrated that neutrons carry no elec-trical charge. He received the Nobel Prize in Physics for that discovery in 1935 and later applied his findings to develop the atomic bomb. As head of the British team that worked in the United States on atomic weapon research—the Manhattan Project—he always hoped that their efforts would be unsuccessful. Many scientists shared his feelings and envisioned atomic power being used for peaceful pur-poses only.

Students can do research to find ways atomic energy is

being used to benefit mankind today or can brainstorm possible applications in the future.

OCTOBER 21, 1833
Birth Date of Alfred Nobel

This Swedish inventor's will provided funds for annual prizes in the fields of physics, chemistry, physiology, medicine, literature, peace, and economics. The man who discovered and manufactured explosives thus hoped to encourage the peaceful use of science and technology. Nobel prizes have been awarded since 1901.

A group of upper-grade students can do research on the following people who have won these awards and report their findings to the class:

Physics: Wilhelm Roentgen for discovering X rays (Germany, 1901); Albert Einstein for work in mathematical physics (Switzerland, 1921).

Chemistry: Frederic and Irene Joliot-Curie for work on new radioactive elements (France, 1935).

Literature: Rudyard Kipling (Great Britain, 1907); Sir Winston Churchill (Great Britain, 1953).

Peace: Theodore Roosevelt for helping end the Russo-Japanese War (United States, 1906); Woodrow Wilson for helping found the League of Nations (United States, 1919); Ralph J. Bunche for mediating in Palestine in 1948–1949 (United States, 1950); Albert Schweitzer for his humanitarian work in Africa (France, 1952); Martin Luther King, Jr. for his work to gain black civil rights by nonviolent direct action (United States, 1964).

OCTOBER 24

The zodiac sign, Scorpio the Scorpion, begins today and ends on November 22. How many children in the class were born under this sign?

OCTOBER 24, 1945
United Nations Day

By presidential proclamation, this date honors the United Nations, which was conceived as an organization to prevent the bloodshed and chaos of another world war. In an attempt to avoid future conflicts, fifty nations drew up the organization's charter, or constitution, in San Francisco on this date; the first formal meeting was held in London in 1946. Today, based in New York City, the United Nations continues to attempt to keep world peace, promote human rights, and serve as a forum where words can take the place of military action.

The United Nations has six main divisions to carry out its programs: The General Assembly, the Security Council, the Trusteeship Council, the International Court of Justice, the Economic and Social Council, and the Secretariat. Students can research the powers allocated to these divisions and present their classmates with information about some of the United Nations' successes and shortcomings.

The United Nations also has many agencies. One of the best known is UNICEF, the United Nations International Children's Emergency Fund. Financed by governments and individuals, UNICEF provides food, medical treatment, raw materials, emergency aid, and funds for education of the world's needy children.

Many books for children have been written about the United Nations; they can be found in school or public libraries. Since the United Nations is an ever-changing organization, caution children to look carefully at the copyright dates in the books they read. (For additional information on the United Nations, see December 10, Human Rights Day.)

OCTOBER 25, 1888
Birth Date of Richard Evelyn Byrd

After graduating from the United States Naval Academy, Richard Byrd devoted his life to aviation and polar exploration. His efforts brought him world acclaim. Listed below are several of his accomplishments:

1925   Commander of a flight over Greenland.
1926   Together with Floyd Bennett, he flew over the North Pole.
1927   Carried first air mail from New York to Paris. Flew over the South Pole.
1934   First man to spend a winter in Antarctica, the coldest place on earth.
1947   Led a thirteen ship exploratory expedition to Antarctica.

Admiral Byrd died in 1957 and was buried at Arlington National Cemetery. He was a direct descendant of William Byrd (1652–1704), one of the earliest plantation owners in Virginia. His brother, Harry F., was a senator from Virginia from 1933–1965.

OCTOBER 26, 1919
Birth Date of Edward W. Brooke

Edward W. Brooke returned to Washington, D. C., the city of his birth, in 1966. His election as a Republican senator from Massachusetts marked a momentous occasion —a black man would sit in the United States Senate for the first time in the twentieth century. Only two other blacks, Hiram Revels (see September 27) and Blanche Kelso Bruce (see March 1) had ever been elected to this important body. While Attorney General of Massachusetts, Brooke had proved his ability as a capable, vote-getting member of his party.

OCTOBER 26, 1927

The first sound motion picture was shown to the public. It was titled *The Jazz Singer* and starred singer Al Jolson.

OCTOBER 27, 1858
Birth Date of Theodore Roosevelt

Twenty-sixth President

Born in:	New York City
Occupation:	Public official, lawyer
President:	1901–1909, Republican
Died:	January 6, 1919
	Oyster Bay, New York

About Roosevelt

🏳 Sickly childhood; spent years building up his health; became a great boxer, outdoorsman, and advocate of exercise.

🏳 Cattle rancher in the Dakota Territory after his first wife's death.

🏳 New York Police Commissioner.

🏳 Led Rough Riders, a volunteer fighting group in the Spanish-American War.

🏳 Became president on September 14, 1901, after assassination of William McKinley.

During His Terms

🏳 Acted against trusts—monopolies that dominated business, industry and even politics.

🏳 Great conservationist—acquired Western lands for public use as national parks.

🏳 Initiated construction of the Panama Canal.

🏳 Won Nobel Peace Prize in 1906 for efforts to end Russo-Japanese War.

OCTOBER 28, 1914
Birth Date of Jonas Salk

In 1952, 58,000 American children contracted the crippling disease of poliomyelitis (polio). Thirteen years later only 121 cases were reported. The miracle of the polio vaccine invented by Dr. Jonas Salk was responsible for this dramatic decrease of a dreaded disease. Dr. Salk dedicated a major portion of his adult life to research on viruses, tiny organisms one millionth of an inch in size. He was on a research team that pioneered in developing a flu vaccine made up of weakened disease germs that cause the body to build up natural immunity, and he envisioned doing the same with the polio virus. After Dr. John Enders of Boston grew polio viruses in a test tube—a feat that won him a Nobel Prize—Salk's team developed a three-step procedure for polio prevention: they grew a virus in a test tube, they killed the virus with disinfectant to create a vaccine, and they injected this substance into people to form antibodies. In 1952 Salk and his family injected themselves with the vaccine to test its effectiveness. Two short years later the vaccine was approved for mass use with over a million people. The result? Polio is now a conquered disease.

OCTOBER 30, 1735
Birth Date of John Adams

Second President
    Born in: Braintree, Massachusetts
    Occupation: Farmer, teacher, lawyer
    President: 1797–1801, Federalist
    Died: July 4, 1826
                    Quincy, Massachusetts

About Adams

🚩 Successfully defended perpetrators of Boston Massacre.

🚩 One of five authors of Declaration of Independence.

🚩 Lived to ninety years of age making him the oldest president.

🚩 His son, John Quincy Adams, became sixth president.

During His Term

🚩 First to live in Washington, D. C., in the White House (1800).

🚩 First United States Navy ship launched, *The United States*.

🚩 Marine Corps was established.

🚩 Library of Congress started.

OCTOBER 31
Halloween

Be on the lookout for goblins or ghosts, pioneers or princesses, witches or wizards, and for tricks or treats, for this is the evening before the feast of All Saints Day initiated by the Roman Catholic Church in the 700s. Tales and customs concerning Halloween characters and events are derived from a wide variety of sources. Children can do research on many aspects of this holiday, one of the most important in the year for girls and boys.

Younger readers will enjoy *Let's Find Out About Halloween* by Paulette Cooper (Watts, 1972), *Halloween* by Helen Borten (T. Y. Crowell, 1965), and *Halloween* by Lillie Patterson (Garrard, 1963). They are easy-to-read books describing some of the history, customs, and familiar celebrations of the day. Middle graders will learn a great deal from *Witches, Pumpkins and Grinning Ghosts* by Edna Barth (Seabury, 1972), which explores the origins of many of the symbols and legends associated with Halloween. Younger children will enjoy hearing parts of the book; most of the sections are short enough to be read in one sitting. Poetry enthusiasts of all ages will find a collection of twenty-three Halloween poems in *Hey How for Halloween!* selected by Lee Bennett Hopkins (Harcourt, 1974).

All children will enjoy creating jack-o'-lanterns. Younger girls and boys will have to be helped with carving the face, but all can scoop out the pumpkin seeds and scrape the insides to make it clean. Seeds can be saved for roasting, eating, and/or planting. Place a candle inside the finished pumpkin. Before the school day ends, turn out the classroom lights, light the jack-o'-lantern, and read the class a spooky poem or story. You might share William Shakespeare's "Song of the Witches" (see April 23, Shakespeare's birthday).

October 31 is also celebrated as National Magic Day, marking the death of the great magician Harry Houdini (see March 24, his birth date). Is there a magician among your students? Have him or her demonstrate some magic tricks for the entire class.

OCTOBER 31, 1864

Nevada became the thirty-sixth state.

ΠOVEMBER

Flower—Chrysanthemum   Birthstone—Topaz

November derives its name from the Latin word *novem* meaning *nine*. November was the ninth month in the Roman calendar.

POEM OF THE MONTH

HAPPY THOUGHTS

The world is so full of a number of things,
I'm sure we should all be as happy as kings.

—Robert Louis Stevenson

NOVEMBER 2, 1734
Birth Date of Daniel Boone

Daniel Boone was an explorer and frontiersman, one of the daring people who constantly wondered what was behind the next mountain. In 1769 he journeyed west from North Carolina. His "highway" through the Cumberland Mountains was an Indian trail, the Warrior's Path. His curiosity and bravery opened up an unsettled area of Kentucky for thousands of pioneers who followed in his footsteps to settle new places. Boone died in Missouri where he had lived to the ripe old age of eighty-six. He was elected to the Hall of Fame in 1915.

Younger children might enjoy mapping an area of their own immediate environment to show streets and familiar landmarks. Older girls and boys can discuss frontier areas remaining on and around our earth. In 1940 James Daugherty's biography *Daniel Boone* (Viking, 1939) won the coveted Newbery Medal. Mature readers will enjoy this book, which tells of Boone's early explorations, the building of the Wilderness Road, and the grim, nine-day siege of Boonesborough.

Upper-graders can hear about Daniel Boone's exciting life on the recording *Daniel Boone: Opening of the Wilderness*. A full-color filmstrip of the same title is also available, accompanied by a teaching guide (both Enrichment).

NOVEMBER 2, 1795
Birth Date of James K. Polk

Eleventh President
    Born in: Mecklenburg County, North Carolina
    Occupation: Lawyer, congressman
    President: 1845–1849, Democrat
    Died: June 15, 1849
             Nashville, Tennessee

About Polk
- Deeply religious.
- Always in poor health.
- First "dark horse" candidate, the result of a Democratic Party stalemate.

During His Term
- War with Mexico.
- Added most territory to the United States after Thomas Jefferson—California, Utah, New Mexico, Nevada, and parts of other Rocky Mountain states.
- United States Naval Academy at Annapolis opened.

NOVEMBER 2, 1865
Birth Date of Warren G. Harding

Twenty-ninth President
    Born in: Corsica, Ohio
    Occupation: Editor, publisher, teacher
    President: 1921–1923, Republican
    Died: August 2, 1923
             San Francisco, California
             Buried in Marion, Ohio

About Harding
- Fun loving, a golfer, and an avid poker player.

During His Term
- Women voted for the first time for president.
- Widespread corruption—Teapot Dome oil scandal.
- Died in office.

NOVEMBER 2, 1889

Two states entered the Union on this date—North Dakota became the thirty-ninth state and South Dakota became the fortieth.

NOVEMBER 3, 1900

The first automobile show opened in New York City at Madison Square Garden. Five years earlier J. Frank Duryea, one of America's leading automobile manufacturing pioneers, won the first United States automobile race held in Chicago, Illinois. He drove his car at an average speed of seven and one-half miles per hour!

Children (and adults) interested in cars will be delighted by *Under the Hood: How Cars Work and How to Keep Them Working* by Robin Lawrie (Pantheon, 1970). It is filled with diagrams and stylized cartoon drawings.

NOVEMBER 4, 1825

> I've got a mule, her name is Sal
> Fifteen miles on the Erie Canal.
> She's a good ol' worker an' a good ol' pal
> Fifteen miles on the Erie Canal.

The refrain of this old folk song was sung by canalboat mule drivers as they traveled along the Erie Canal, which opened on this date. The Erie Canal is a waterway stretching across northern New York State; it was the first major waterway to be constructed in the United States. It linked the Hudson River with Lake Erie to provide a transportation route between the Eastern Seaboard and the Great Lakes.

NOVEMBER 5, 1958

Shirley Chisholm became the first black woman to be elected to the House of Representatives.

NOVEMBER 6

1792—George Washington was reelected president of the United States.

1860—Abraham Lincoln was elected president of the United States.

1869—The first formal intercollegiate football game was played between Princeton and Rutgers at New Brunswick, New Jersey.

NOVEMBER 8, 1889

Montana became the forty-first state.

NOVEMBER 9, 1906

President Theodore Roosevelt sailed on a United States battleship for the Panama Canal Zone, becoming the first United States president to leave the country while serving in office. Times have certainly changed! Today it is quite common for the president to make trips abroad. Encourage children to look for current events articles that describe presidential journeys and/or discuss the purposes of foreign travel for a nation's leader.

NOVEMBER 11
Veterans Day

On November 11, 1918, an armistice was signed. World War I was over. It wasn't until November 1921, however, that Armistice Day was declared a national legal holiday by Congress to honor those who gave their lives in World War I. It was at this time that an unknown soldier was buried in a bomb in Arlington National Cemetery in Arlington, Virginia, across the Potomac River from Washing, D. C. In June 1954, President Dwight D. Eisenhower signed a bill designating the day as Veterans Day to honor also the dead of World War II and the Korean War. Today Veterans Day is celebrated on different dates. Check your calendar to see when it comes this year.

NOVEMBER 11, 1889

Washington became the forty-second state.

NOVEMBER 12, 1815
Birth Date of Elizabeth Cady Stanton

American women were angered when the Fifteenth Amendment to the United States Constitution was passed because it granted former slaves the right to vote but continued to limit the vote to males. The National Woman Suffrage Association was formed in 1869 to secure that right. Ms. Stanton was elected president of the organization, which became one of the foremost forces to educate and agitate for female voting rights. Ms. Stanton worked closely with Lucretia Mott and Susan B. Anthony (see February 15).

Finally on August 26, 1920, with the ratification of the Nineteenth Amendment, American women won the right to vote and have since played a vital part in the political life of the nation.

Middle graders will glean a great deal of information from *An Album of Women in American History* by Claire R. and Leonard W. Ingraham (Watts, 1972).

NOVEMBER 12, 1840
Birth Date of François Auguste Rodin

> Nothing is ugly that has life. Whatever suggests human emotion, whether of grief, or pain, goodness or anger, hate or love, has its individual seal of beauty.
>
> —Rodin

Paris-born Rodin's statement expresses this great sculptor's belief in the humanistic nature of art. He started his career as a stonemason, progressed to working upon adornments for building facades, and culminated as a sculptor, creating realistic, free-standing figures. Among his many great works are *The Thinker, Bronze Age, Hugo, Balzac,* and *The Burghers of Calais.* His works are displayed in museums throughout the world. There is a Rodin Museum in Philadelphia and in Paris.

NOVEMBER
Election Day

Ancient Greeks voted with colored stones—black signified no, white, yes. Using this device, a select portion of the male population was permitted to express preferences in civic affairs. Many colonial Americans voted similarly, using different colored corn kernels to express their wishes. The term *ballot* originated in the republics of Venice and Florence where colored balls, *ballotta*, were used for voting.

In 1888 the Australian ballot, a paper ballot listing candidates' names, was first used in the United States. It insured greater secrecy for voters. Today Americans over eighteen years of age have the right to vote when most national, state, and local elections take place on the first Tuesday after the first Monday in November. Young readers can learn more about the event in *Election Day* by Mary Kay Phelan (T. Y. Crowell, 1967).

NOVEMBER
Children's Book Week

Since 1919 Children's Book Week has been sponsored by the Children's Book Council. The week-long event is designed to invite students to expand their horizons through reading. The Children's Book Council (67 Irving Place, New York, N.Y. 10003) is a year-round source of information about children's literature. A list of the Council's publications and current order forms may be obtained by sending a 10¢ stamped, self-addressed #10 envelope. An important publication of the Council is *The Calendar*. Published quarterly, it features timely articles and lists free and/or inexpensive materials such as posters, bookmarks, and biographical sketches of authors and illustrators. A one-time $5 fee will put you on the mailing list forever!

Children's Book Week is a good time to visit or revisit the school and/or public library. Plan ahead to have the librarian talk to the children about books and other items available in the library. Your class might enjoy engaging in a special activity to help celebrate this week. An ongoing group project can be constructing a class bookworm. Cut circles from different colors of paper. Make the face of the bookworm on one circle and hang it on a wall. After children read a new book, they write the title of the book, author, and his or her name on a circle, and attach it to the head to make the body of the bookworm. Children will enjoy watching their bookworm grow and grow as the school year progresses.

NOVEMBER 13, 1850
Birth Date of Robert Louis Balfour Stevenson

Born in Edinburgh, Scotland, the only son of an engineer, Stevenson was afflicted with a lung disease as a child and was often confined to bed. Throughout his childhood he required the care of a nursemaid. She was Alison Cunningham to whom Stevenson dedicated his *A Child's Garden of Verses* (1885). Besides poetry, he wrote several classic novels: *Treasure Island* (1883), *Kidnapped* (1886), and *The Strange Case of Dr. Jekyll and Mr. Hyde* (1886). In 1880 Stevenson and his family settled in Samoa, an island in the Pacific Ocean, where he lived until his death on December 3, 1895.

There are many editions of *A Child's Garden of Verses*. Two particularly handsome volumes are illustrated by Brian Wildsmith (Watts, 1966) and Tasha Tudor (Walck, 1947). The November poem of the month, "Happy Thoughts," is in this collection and can be shared with children of all ages. Older girls and boys can read a wide selection of Stevenson's work in *Poems of Robert Louis Stevenson* selected by Helen Plotz (T. Y. Crowell, 1973).

NOVEMBER 14, 1765
Birth Date of Robert Fulton

Born in Lancaster County, Pennsylvania, Fulton first intended to become a painter, but at age twenty-nine he became interested in canal engineering. Three years later he proposed the idea of a submarine, which he finally built in 1800. The next year he met Robert R. Livingston, a man who for two decades held a monopoly on steamboat navigation in the state of New York. Together they planned the construction of a steamboat which became a reality in 1807.

Clara Ingram Judson's *Boat Builder: The Story of Robert Fulton* (Scribner, 1940) is a biography that can be read by middle-grade youngsters.

NOVEMBER 16, 1907

Oklahoma became the forty-sixth state.

NOVEMBER 18, 1789
Birth Date of Louis Jacques Mandé Daguerre

Louis Daguerre, a French painter and physicist, announced the invention of the daguerreotype, the first practical method of photography, in 1838. His discovery has been acclaimed as one of the world's greatest inventions. This might be a good day to take one or several photographs of the class. An exciting project is to have children create their own filmstrips or slides. Children can work individually or in groups to draw art and write or tape scripts. A helpful kit, which includes filmstrip and slide film, special pencils, and filmstrip containers, is *Draw Your Own Filmstrip and Slide Kit* (Scholastic Audio-Visual).

NOVEMBER 19, 1831
Birth Date of James A. Garfield

Twentieth President
>Born in: Orange, Ohio
>Occupation: Lawyer, congressman
>President: 1881, Republican
>Died: September 19, 1881
>   Elberon, New Jersey
>   Buried in Cleveland, Ohio

About Garfield
🏳 Worked as a canal boatman, janitor, teacher of ancient languages, college president, preacher, and Union army general, besides practicing law.

During His Term
🏳 Opposed the spoils system of granting federal jobs to political friends.

🏳 Shot by a disappointed job seeker in a Washington railroad station; he lingered for seventy-nine days before dying.

NOVEMBER 19, 1863

Abraham Lincoln delivered the Gettysburg Address at the dedication of a national cemetery on the battlefield where so many soldiers had died the summer before during the three-day battle of Gettysburg (see July 1). Lincoln's speech began with the historic words:

>Fourscore and seven years ago our fathers brought forth on this continent a new nation, conceived in Liberty, and dedicated to the proposition that all men are created equal. . . .

[47]

The entire speech consisted of only three hundred words, but it has come down through history as one of the most noble expressions of what democracy means.

The complete text of the speech can be found in *Freedom Encyclopedia: American Liberties in the Making* by Frances Cavanah (Rand McNally, 1968).

NOVEMBER 20, 1925
Birth Date of Robert Francis Kennedy

> If we cannot open to youth a sense of possibility, we will have only ourselves to blame for their disillusionment; and with their disillusionment lies the danger—for we rely on our youth for all our hopes of a better future—and thus in a real and direct sense, for the very meaning of our own lives.
>
> —Senator Robert F. Kennedy

Robert F. Kennedy shared the vision of a New Frontier held by his brother, John Fitzgerald Kennedy, the thirty-fifth President of the United States (see May 29, 1917). Bobby, as he was popularly known, served in his brother's administration as Attorney General, helping to shape a new approach to poverty, civil rights, and foreign affairs. After John Kennedy's death, Robert continued to serve the nation; he was elected senator from New York State in 1964; in 1968 he entered the Democratic Party's presidential primary. While campaigning in Los Angeles, where he scored a victory, he was assassinated. The death of the two Kennedys has had a profound effect upon the nation's political affairs.

Older readers can read about the man in *Robert F. Kennedy: Man Who Dared to Dream* by Charles P. Graves (Garrard, 1970).

NOVEMBER 21, 1789

North Carolina was the twelfth state to ratify the Constitution.

NOVEMBER 23

The zodiac sign, Sagittarius the Archer, begins today and ends on December 21. How many children in the class were born under this sign?

NOVEMBER 23, 1804
Birth Date of Franklin Pierce

Fourteenth President

Born in:	Hillsboro, New Hampshire
Occupation:	Lawyer
President:	1853–1857, Democrat
Died:	October 8, 1869
	Concord, New Hampshire

About Pierce

🏳 Childhood of wealth, good education, and politically prominent family.

🏳 Served in the Mexican War.

🏳 Won Democratic nomination on forty-ninth ballot as a compromise "dark horse."

During His Term

🏳 His failure to solve slavery issue led to the formation of a new Republican Party by his opponents.

🏳 Opened first World's Fair in the United States, the Crystal Palace Exposition in New York City in July 1853.

NOVEMBER 24, 1784
Birth Date of Zachary Taylor

Twelfth President

Born in: Orange County, Virginia
Occupation: Soldier
President: 1849–1850, Whig
Died: Washington, D. C.
July 9, 1850
Buried in Springfield, Kentucky

About Taylor
- Frontier background.
- Little formal education.
- General in war against Mexico.
- Nicknamed Old Rough and Ready.

During His Term
- Firmly against spread of slavery; hated politics and appeasement of south.
- Pastured his horse, Whitey, on White House lawn.
- Died sixteen months after taking office.

NOVEMBER 29, 1832
Birth Date of Louisa May Alcott

Born in Germantown, Pennsylvania, Louisa May Alcott lived most of her life in New England. Ralph Waldo Emerson and Henry David Thoreau were among her friends, and Nathaniel Hawthorne was a neighbor. Because her father, a philosopher, was a poor provider, Ms. Alcott began early in life to provide for her family. As a child she earned money by making dolls' clothes. Later she taught school, which she hated! Eventually she turned to writing. Her first published book, *Flower Fables,* appeared in 1854; this was a collection of fairy stories originally told to Emerson's daughter. While serving voluntarily as a nurse in the Civil War, she contracted typhoid. Her first major book, *Hospital Sketches* (1863), was written after this experience. Later several of her stories were published in *Atlantic Monthly*. Because of these she was asked to write a book "for girls." At first she refused the offer "not liking girls, preferring boys" but because she needed money, she wrote the novel, *Little Women*, which is quite autobiographical. After she handed in the manuscript, her publisher thought it quite unacceptable. Fortunately he allowed the children in his family to read it. They loved it, it was published (1868–69), and a classic was born—the first great novel for children dealing with family life.

Other books based on Ms. Alcott's early life experiences followed such as *Little Men* (1871) and *Jo's Boys* (1886), but none were as popular with children as *Little Women*. There are now many editions of the volume in both hardcover and paperback. A particularly handsome one is illustrated by the Caldecott Award winning artist Barbara Cooney (T. Y. Crowell, 1955). If you have students in the upper grades who haven't tasted the joys of this novel, steer them to it. They will also enjoy reading the biography of the author *Invincible Louisa* by Cornelia Meigs (Little, Brown, 1933; also in paper, Scholastic Book Services). This book won the 1934 Newbery Medal and still is popular with upper-grade readers.

NOVEMBER 30, 1874
Birth Date of Winston Churchill

Reporter, army officer, prime minister, world statesman, and architect of the policy of resistance to communist expansion (Cold War) are some of the roles this English political leader filled during his active life. Winston Churchill's cigar-smoking countenance, his V for victory handsignal, and his bulldog appearance were known throughout the Western world when he served as England's Prime Minister during the years when Britain and the United States were allies during the dark days of World War II. As a young man he had joined the army because his parents thought him a poor student; he was a reporter during the Boer War in Africa and was a prolific writer and amateur painter.

History-minded students can find many vignettes about his life and times for sharing. Mature readers can learn more about the man in *Winston Churchill and the Story of Two World Wars* by Olivia Coolidge (Houghton, 1960) and *The Complete Life of Winston Churchill* by Leonard Wibberley (Farrar, Straus, 1968).

NOVEMBER
Thanksgiving Day

The Pilgrims landed in the New World on December 21, 1620, after an arduous voyage from England. Governor William Bradford of the Plymouth Colony proclaimed a day of Thanksgiving a year later, a day that was shared with the Indians. Thanksgiving Day has been celebrated on different dates in various states and was mainly a New England holiday. Sara Josepha Hale was the first to suggest that Thanksgiving be a national patriotic holiday. Ms. Hale was the editor of a popular women's magazine, *Godey's Ladies Book*, and for almost twenty years she campaigned through editorials and letters to the president and state governors. She finally won the support of President Abraham Lincoln, who in 1864 issued a proclamation making the last Thursday in November Thanksgiving Day.

Each year during the last two weeks in November there is a daily re-creation of the Pilgrims' original Thanksgiving feast at the Plimoth Plantation at Plymouth, Massachusetts. Visitors can see people engaged in the everyday tasks of a seventeenth century farming community. A full-scale reproduction of *The Mayflower* is berthed nearby and open to the public.

Ideas for activities to celebrate Thanksgiving can be gleaned from many books. For younger readers suggest *Thanksgiving Day* by Robert Merrill Bartlett (T. Y. Crowell, 1965), *The Thanksgiving Story* by Alice Dalgliesh (Scribner, 1954), and *Thanksgiving* by Lee Wyndham (Garrard, 1963). Middle-grade children will enjoy *It's Time for Thanksgiving* by Elizabeth Hough Sechrist and Janette Woolsey (Macrae Smith, 1957). The history of the holiday is followed by stories, plays, poems, games, and recipes.

Decorate the classroom bulletin boards with the attractive Pilgrim Portfolio (Scholastic Book Services), a collection of ten prints, paintings, and sketches showing the early days of the Pilgrims. It can be used with the book *Pilgrim Stories* by Elvajean Hall (Scholastic Book Services, paper), which features episodes about Pilgrim beginnings in England and Holland, *The Mayflower*, and the first year in the New World.

NOVEMBER/DECEMBER
Hanukkah

Hanukkah, or the Festival of Lights, lasts eight days. It begins on the twenty-fifth day of the Hebrew month of Kislev. On the Roman calendar, this falls at the end of November or some time during the month of December. The holiday is a joyous occasion commemorating the

Hebrew victory over Syria's oppressive King Antiochus, in which the Maccabees recaptured the temple of Jerusalem.

The Menorah, a candlestick, is an important symbol of the event. The Menorah has nine cups for candles. Eight candles represent the eight days the oil burned during the first Hanukkah. Hebrew legend states that the Maccabees were miraculously able to burn one day's oil supply for eight days once their temple was cleansed of Antiochus' pagan statues. The candlelight reminds the Jewish people of their fight to pray to their own God in their own way. The ninth cup holds the shamos candle. *Shamos* means *servant* in Hebrew. Each night the shamos is lit first and then used to light the other candles. One candle is lit each night until all eight burn brightly. Children receive small gifts on each of the eight days, sing songs, and play games.

A top-like toy, the dreidel, might be shown to the children. It is closely associated with the holiday, and children will be fascinated to discover its role in the Hanukkah ritual. On each side is one Hebrew letter: Nun, or N; Gimel, or G; Hei, or H; Shin, or Sh. These are the first letters of the Hebrew words *Nes Godal Hayah Sham* meaning *a great miracle happened there*. Several children can demonstrate to the class how to play dreidel. Each player has a chance to spin the dreidel, and how it falls determines the outcome of the game.

Many children confuse Hanukkah with Christmas. This would be a good time to have individuals or small groups plan a report on the significance of each of the holidays to share with the class. *Hanukkah* by Norma Simon (T. Y. Crowell, 1966) tells the complete story of this holiday with simplicity. A more detailed account appears in *A Great Miracle: The Story of Hanukkah* by Betty Morrow (Harvey House, 1968).

DECEMBER

Flower—Narcissus   Birthstone—Turquoise

The name of the last month of the year comes from the Latin word *decem* meaning *tenth*. December was the tenth month in the Roman calendar.

POEM OF THE MONTH

SING HEY!

Sing hey! Sing hey!
For Christmas Day;
Twine mistletoe and holly,
For a friendship glows
In winter snows,
And so let's all be jolly!

—Anonymous

DECEMBER 3, 1818

Illinois became the twenty-first state.

DECEMBER 5, 1782
Birth Date of Martin Van Buren

Eighth President

Born in:	Kinderhook, New York
Occupation:	Lawyer
President:	1837–1841, Democrat
Died:	July 24, 1862
	Kinderhook, New York

About Van Buren
- Built New York political machine.
- Vice-president during Jackson's second term.
- Helped Jackson form Democratic Party.
- Presidential candidate again in 1848 for Free Soil Party.

During His Term
- First "machine elected" president.
- Economic depression occurred.
- Lost election of 1840 to William Henry Harrison—dirtiest campaign in history.

DECEMBER 6, 1770
Birth Date of Ludwig van Beethoven

Beethoven's early musical compositions embodied the classical style prevalent in the royal courts of Europe. Born in Bonn, Germany, the composer studied briefly with Haydn and Mozart after moving to Vienna, Austria. He composed chamber music, symphonic pieces, and piano masterpieces that expressed his feelings for humanity and foreshadowed the development of nineteenth century romantic music. Despite the fact that he became totally deaf early in life, the great master continued to compose and produce many works until his death in 1827.

Play a Beethoven selection for the children today. Recently his "Ode to Joy" from his *Ninth Symphony* has become a Christmas favorite. The song has been recorded by Miguel Rios, a young Spanish pop star, among others. Also in a light vein is Beethoven's famous *Moonlight Sonata*. *Beethoven: Master Musician* by Madeleine Goss (Holt, 1946) and *Ludwig Beethoven and the Chiming Tower Bells* by Opal Wheeler (Dutton, 1942) are two biographies for mature readers.

DECEMBER 7, 1787

Delaware was the first state to ratify the Constitution.

DECEMBER 7, 1941

Pearl Harbor was attacked. President Franklin Delano Roosevelt called this a day of infamy in which Japanese bombers destroyed the military and naval base on the island of Oahu in the Hawaiian Islands. The sudden attack, carried out without warning, plunged the United States into World War II. Its perpetrators, the Japanese military and naval hierarchy, were punished after the war.

Students might enjoy discovering more about the Hawaiian Islands. Subjects of interest could include their volcanic nature, their history since 1778 when they were discovered by an Englishman, James Cook, who named them the Sandwich Islands, and their present status as our newest state—the fiftieth.

DECEMBER 8, 1765
Birth Date of Eli Whitney

Farmer, part-time college student, teacher, inventor, munitions maker—these all describe Eli Whitney, a pioneer in the development of modern industrial methods. Born in Westboro, Massachusetts, Whitney helped on his father's farm and in spare moments worked his way through Yale University. A lifelong fascination with things mechanical prompted him to manufacture nails. His later invention of the cotton engine, or gin, revolutionized the cotton industry. It separated cotton fibers from seeds rapidly; previously this had been done by hand, a slow, tedious process. Whitney patented the machine on March 14, 1794, but had to sue to secure his rights. He won the case but never reaped much money from his invention. In the early 1800s, he turned to manufacturing guns for the United States Army and pioneered the mass production of rifles with interchangeable parts. Mass production techniques are now utilized in all modern manufacturing.

Eli Whitney: Great Inventor by Newbery Award winner Jean Lee Latham (Garrard, 1963), is a fine introductory biography for young readers.

DECEMBER 10
Human Rights Day

On December 10, 1948, the United Nations produced an international definition of the rights of man known as the Universal Declaration of Human Rights. Since then every December 10 has been designated Human Rights Day. The Declaration is considered one of the finest accomplishments of the United Nations. It sets forth the following human rights as goals for all governments to work toward:

- The right of individuals to life, liberty, and security.
- The right of everyone to an education and to equality before the law.
- The right of each person to move about freely, to worship as he chooses, to associate freely with other people, and to have access to information in his search for understanding.
- The right of everyone to be a citizen of a country and to work under favorable conditions with equal pay for equal work.
- The right to marry and raise a family.

The Declaration has influenced the shaping of the constitutions of new countries and has helped to change the practices of some countries toward slavery, forced labor, and the rights of women and children.

Human Rights Day by Aileen Fisher and Olive Rabe (T. Y. Crowell, 1966) explains the significance of this day in terms that younger readers will easily grasp. For additional information on the United Nations, see October 24.

DECEMBER 10, 1817

Mississippi became the twentieth state.

DECEMBER 10, 1830
Birth Date of Emily Dickinson

> To live is so startling it leaves little time for anything else.
>
> —from a letter by Emily Dickinson

Though Emily Dickinson wrote over 1,700 poems, only six were printed while she was alive. She preserved the others in hand-sewn leather booklets. She was born in Amherst, Massachusetts, and lived there all her life. She began writing verse in 1860. Her main themes dealt with love, death, and nature.

The following books, all for mature readers, contain many interesting facts about this beloved poet: *I'm Nobody! Who Are You?* by Edna Barth (Seabury, 1971), *We Dickinsons* by Aileen Fisher and Olive Rabe (Atheneum, 1965), *A Letter to the World: Poems for Young Dickinson: Her Letter to the World* by Polly Longsworth (T. Y. Crowell, 1965).

DECEMBER 10, 1909

Red Cloud, last of the great Sioux chieftans, was buried in the Mission Cemetery on the hill above the Red Cloud Indian School in Pine Ridge, South Dakota. There is no record of his birth date. In the course of his eighty years, Red Cloud had witnessed the extermination of his people. The Sioux nation occupied the north-central portion of today's United States. They were driven to desperation by the seizures of their lands and the slaughter of their food supply, the bison. Many battles were fought as whites poured West after the Civil War. At the most famous, the Battle of Little Bighorn in Montana in 1876, Sitting Bull defeated General George Custer's troops. Today, there are almost one million Americans of Indian descent. Half of them live in poverty on reservations where squalid conditions have brought them into the headlines once again.

DECEMBER 11, 1816

Indiana became the nineteenth state.

DECEMBER 12, 1787

Pennsylvania was the second state to ratify the Constitution.

DECEMBER 12, 1901

Guglielmo Marconi sent the first radio signal across the Atlantic Ocean from Cornwall, England, to Newfoundland in North America. The work of Marconi, an Italian engineer, has saved countless lives at sea and enabled people to communicate instantly over vast distances via radio wave transmission. His company used wireless radio to bridge the English Channel to send messages from Britain to France in 1899. Because of his pioneering efforts, Marconi was awarded the Nobel Prize in Physics in 1909. Today's communications industry is possible thanks to the many contributions Marconi made to radio and telephone broadcasting.

DECEMBER 13, 1577

Sir Frances Drake started a voyage around the world to become the first Englishman to sail around the globe. With

160 men and five ships Drake spent the next three years sailing around South America to California, which he claimed for his country, then across the Pacific and Indian Oceans, and finally up the coast of Africa. Students can use a world map to trace Drake's route and see the enormous distances involved.

DECEMBER 14, 1819

Alabama became the twenty-second state.

DECEMBER 14, 1911

Roald Amundsen's dog sled expedition reached the South Pole, the farthest south one can go from the equator. The Norwegian-born explorer achieved a lifelong ambition on the frozen wasteland of the Antarctic continent, a region where the earth's coldest temperature of 102° below Fahrenheit was recorded in 1957–1958. Amundsen's feat came after he had lost the race to the North Pole; an American, Robert E. Peary, reached that site in 1909 (see April 6).

Children can compile a series of polar facts to share with others by reading about Peary, Amundsen, Robert Scott, Richard Byrd, and other polar explorers, Eskimo life in the Arctic, and penguin behavior on the Antarctic continent. A good reference book for middle graders is *All About the Arctic and Antarctic* by the 1941 Newbery Award winning author Armstrong Sperry (Random, 1957).

DECEMBER 16, 1773

Boston's harbor became a giant teapot in an event known as the Boston Tea Party. As a crowd of spectators watched, the Sons of Liberty, a patriot group disguised as Indians, deliberately dumped 342 cases of tea into the waters. This illegal action was a protest against a tax placed on tea by the British Parliament. Although the tax was insignificant, colonial citizens felt compelled to make a gesture of defiance against "outside" interference in their affairs. (See also April 22, 1774.)

Upper-grade youngsters can read about this historical drama in *The Story of the Boston Tea Party* by Mary Kay Phelan (T. Y. Crowell, 1973).

DECEMBER 18, 1787

New Jersey became the third state to ratify the Constitution.

DECEMBER 18, 1865

The Thirteenth Amendment was ratified as part of the United States Constitution. Starting with the words, "Neither slavery or involuntary servitude . . .," this historic addition to the Constitution brought an end to the cruel system of forced labor that had been practiced for over 200 years in the United States.

Great Slave Narratives selected and introduced by Arna Bontemps (Beacon Press, 1969) is a fine volume for teacher reference.

DECEMBER 21
First Day of Winter

For some suggestions on welcoming the winter season, see the entry for September 21.

DECEMBER 22

The zodiac sign, Capricorn the Goat, begins today and ends on January 20. Find out how many children in the class were born under this sign.

DECEMBER 25
Christmas Day

Christmas Day celebrates the birthday of Jesus Christ, born nearly two thousand years ago in Bethlehem. The Christmas holiday is celebrated in many parts of the world. In some countries Christmas greetings are said in this way:

		Pronunciation
Danish:	*Glaedelig Jul*	GLA-da-lig U-el
Finnish:	*Hauskaa Joulua*	HAUS-ka U-loo-a
French:	*Joyeux Nöel*	jo-YEH no-EL
German:	*Fröhliche Weinachten*	FRO-leek-eh Vly-nak-tehn
Greek:	*Kala Christougenna*	ka-LA Chris-TOU-yeh-na
Italian:	*Buon Natale*	boo-ON na-TA-leh
Norwegian/ Swedish:	*God Jul*	Gud U-el
Portuguese:	*Feliz Natal*	feh-LEES na-TAL
Russian:	*S Rozhdyestvom Khristovym*	S Ro-zhdye-STVOM Krist-TOYM
Spanish:	*Feliz Navidad*	feh-LEES na-VI-dad

There are many titles in the school or public library about this joyous holiday. Several for younger readers are *Christmas* by Barbara Cooney (T. Y. Crowell, 1967) and

Christmas Feasts and Festivals (Garrard, 1968) and *Christmas in America* (Garrard, 1969), both by Lillie Patterson.

For older readers suggest *Holly, Reindeer, and Colored Lights: The Story of Christmas Symbols* by Edna Barth (Seabury, 1971) and *It's Time for Christmas* by Elizabeth Hough Sechrist and Janette Woolsey (Macrae Smith, 1959). An excellent book for teacher reference is *Christmas Holiday Book* by Yorke Henderson and others (Parents', 1972). Here you will find stories, music, poems, and recipes. Poetry readers of all ages will enjoy *Sing Hey for Christmas Day!* selected by Lee Bennett Hopkins (Harcourt, 1975).

DECEMBER 25, 1642
Birth Date of Sir Isaac Newton

English-born Isaac Newton is often remembered with the true anecdote about his discovery of gravity while sitting under an apple tree. The apple's fall initiated his monumental investigation of gravity—the mysterious force that holds the universe together. While attending Cambridge University, where he was a mediocre student, often spending hours under apple trees, Newton made three of his most important contributions to science: the invention of calculus, his theory of gravitation, and the discovery of the spectrum—a pioneering effort in a new field. Newton's accomplishments won him a professorship at Cambridge as well as world fame. He died on March 20, 1727, in Kensington, England.

Gravity All Around by Tillie S. Pine and Joseph Levine (McGraw-Hill, 1963) provides a simple explanation of this concept and offers youngsters ideas for simple experiments that they can handle. Upper-graders can read about the lives and achievements of Galileo and Newton in *Universe of Galileo and Newton* by William Bixby (Harper, 1964).

[65]

DECEMBER 25, 1821
Birth Date of Clara Barton

Clara Barton's lifelong interest in the nursing profession made her internationally famous as the founder and leading spirit of the American Red Cross. This organization was founded on May 21, 1881.

Young readers can read about her work in *Clara Barton: Soldier of Mercy* by Mary Catherine Rose (Garrard, 1960); older boys and girls can read *Clara Barton: Founder of the Red Cross* by Helen Dore Boylston (Random House, 1955), which emphasizes her work as a Civil War nurse.

DECEMBER 27, 1822
Birth Date of Louis Pasteur

What are the most numerous living things? Bacteria, of course. They are one-celled organisms that are both harmful and helpful to man.

Louis Pasteur, the French chemist, pioneered in the discovery and control of these microscopic life forms. His studies of fermentation in wine led him to conclude that the process was caused by airborne bacteria. Pasteur's name is closely associated with immunization or vaccination—producing resistance to disease by injecting weakened germ cultures. Pasteurization—the killing of harmful germs by heating—and the development of a cure for rabies are also credited to the scientist.

Have a group of children draw pictures of the three bacteria types: round, rod shaped, and spiral shaped. Another topic for investigation is how bacteria help man. Encourage children to look for the word *pasteurized* on milk containers and other dairy products.

DECEMBER 28, 1846

Iowa became the twenty-ninth state.

DECEMBER 28, 1856
Birth Date of Woodrow Wilson

Twenty-eighth President

Born in:	Staunton, Virginia
Occupation:	Educator, lawyer
President:	1913–1921, Democrat
Died:	February 3, 1924
	Washington, D. C.

About Wilson
- Only president with a Ph.D. degree.
- President of Princeton University.
- Writer of political science texts.

During His Terms
- Started press conferences.
- Women obtained the right to vote.
- United States entered World War I.
- Pioneered for peace and for the creation of the League of Nations.
- Suffered crippling stroke at the end of his term, leaving the nation with a disabled president.

DECEMBER 29, 1808
Birth Date of Andrew Johnson

Seventeenth President

Born in:	Raleigh, North Carolina
Occupation:	Tailor, public official
President:	1865–1869, Democrat
Died:	July 31, 1875
	Carter Station, Tennessee

About Johnson

☰ Because of his bleak poverty, he was called "a working man's champion."

☰ The only Southern senator to stick with the Union; twenty-one others left.

☰ Became Lincoln's vice-president on March 4, 1865, one month before the president was assassinated.

During His Term

☰ Conflict with radical Republicans over the treatment of the defeated Confederate states and alleged misuse of presidential power led to an impeachment trial in which the Senate vote on removing him failed by one vote.

☰ Alaska purchased from Russia in 1867; the cold area was called "Johnson's polar bear garden," reflecting its lack of appeal.

DECEMBER 29, 1845

Texas became the twenty-eighth state.

DECEMBER 29, 1876
Birth Date of Pablo Casals

The name Casals is synonymous with the cello, an instrument this musician mastered early in his life. Born in a Catalan town in Spain, forty miles from Barcelona, Casals was introduced to the flute, piano, violin, and cello by his father, who was a choirmaster. The young Casals could sing in tune before he could talk clearly; at age five he was a soprano in a church choir. In the 1930s he chose self-exile from his native Spain rather than accept Franco's totalitarian regime. His cello performances, particularly Bach solos, won him world acclaim. In 1956 he adopted

Puerto Rico as his home and organized an annual music festival on the island. He died there in 1973 at age ninety-seven.

DECEMBER 30, 1865
Birth Date of Rudyard Kipling

Although Rudyard Kipling wrote several successful adult novels and a large amount of poetry, it was his stories for children that earned him an international and lasting reputation. These include the popular *Jungle Books* (1894, 1895) and *Just-So Stories* (1902). Kipling's writings about nature and the habitats of animals, particularly his tales in the *Jungle Books*, are very accurate. He was born in India where his father was a British official. When he was six he was brought to England for his education. School life was an unhappy experience, and he drew upon it later in several books including *Stalky and Company* (1899). In 1882 he returned to India as a journalist. He married an American woman and lived in Vermont for four years. In later life he became champion of the British Empire. Kipling was England's first winner of the Nobel Prize for Literature in 1907.

Children still enjoy Kipling's stories. The *Jungle Books* contain the classic tales of Mowgli, a boy adopted by a wolf pack and taught the way of the jungle, and "Rikki-Tikki-Tavi," a tale about a mongoose. Younger girls and boys will delight in hearing *Just-So Stories*, which include "The Elephant's Child," "How the Camel Got His Hump," and "How the Leopard Got His Spots." With older children these tales might spark creative writing; have them make up their own "how-thes"! The tales also adapt easily to puppet plays. Two handsome editions of Kipling's work, both illustrated by Caldecott Award winning artists, are

The Elephant's Child illustrated by Leonard Weisgard (Walker, 1970) and *Just-So Stories* illustrated by Nicolas (Doubleday, 1952).

DECEMBER 31

> Ring out the old, ring in the new,
>   Ring, happy bells, across the snow:
>   The year is going, let him go;
> Ring out the false, ring in the true.
> —Alfred, Lord Tennyson
> from "Ring Out, Wild Bells"

Tonight is the night when Western peoples celebrate the coming of the New Year. It is usually marked by parties, jolly celebrations, and New Year's resolutions.

JANUARY

Flower—Carnation   Birthstone—Garnet

The first month receives its name from the Latin *Januarius*, which was derived from *janua* meaning *door*. The word came from the name of the god Janus, whom ancient Romans believed opened the gates of heaven to release daylight and closed them when dusk arrived. The god also looked both to the past and to the future.

POEM OF THE MONTH

Beautiful Soup! Who cares for fish,
Game, or any other dish?
Who would not give all else for two p
ennyworth only of beautiful Soup?
   Beau-ootiful Soo----oop!
   Beau-ootiful Soo----oop!
Soo-----oop of the e----e----evening,
   Beautiful, beautif--FUL SOUP!

Beautiful Soup, so rich and green,
Waiting in a hot tureen!
Who for such dainties would not stoop?
Soup of the evening, beautiful Soup!
   Beau-ootiful Soo----oop!
   Beau-ootiful Soo----oop!
Soo----oop of the e----e----evening,
   Beautiful, beautiful Soup!

—Lewis Carroll

JANUARY 1
New Year's Day

Happy New Year!

No one really knows when the custom of celebrating the New Year began, but New Year's Day is a holiday that is celebrated all over the world—often at different times. (For example, see September/October, Jewish New Year; January/February, Chinese New Year; Iranian New Year, March 21.) In America, of course, the annual celebration takes place on January 1 and usually starts well before midnight on December 31.

When the children return to school from their winter

recess, discuss New Year's resolutions with them. Each child can write out one or several resolutions that she or he would like to keep during the new year. Place them on a bulletin board display entitled "Our New Year's Resolutions." Decorate the board with balloons and leftover New Year's Eve paraphernalia—party hats, streamers, and the like. Children who want to know more about the various ways people celebrate the New Year today and throughout history will enjoy reading *New Year's Day* by Lynn Groh (Garrard, 1964), an easy-to-read but detailed account of the holiday.

JANUARY 1, 1863

The Emancipation Proclamation was signed. This document was conceived as a military expedient rather than as a moral declaration ending slavery. Six months prior to issuing the Proclamation, President Abraham Lincoln warned the rebelling states that such an act was forthcoming; as commander in chief, the president was fearful of the military use the South could make of its slave manpower. The Emancipation Proclamation freed only slaves held in seceded states. Nevertheless, it set the stage for the Thirteenth Amendment to the Constitution, which outlawed slavery in the entire United States (see December 18). Abolitionists, including the black leader Frederick Douglass, hailed the Proclamation as a historic step in the fight for freedom.

Older girls and boys might discuss President Lincoln's attitude toward slavery in an open-ended fashion, since much interest has recently focused upon whether he really was anxious to end slavery. A resource book for older readers is *Lincoln and the Emancipation Proclamation, January 1, 1863: The Document That Turned the Civil War into a Fight for Freedom* by Frank B. Latham (Watts, 1969; also in paper).

JANUARY 2, 1788

Georgia became the fourth state to ratify the Constitution.

JANUARY 2, 1893

The first commemorative postage stamp was issued by the Post Office Department. It was called the Columbian issue in honor of the four hundredth anniversary of the discovery of America. Student stamp collectors might bring in some commemorative stamps to show and discuss with the class.

JANUARY 3, 1959

Alaska became the forty-ninth state.

JANUARY 4, 1785
Birth Date of Jakob Grimm

Both Jakob and his brother Wilhelm Karl (1786–1859) were born in Hanau, Germany. Following in their father's footsteps, both boys began to study law, but they also had a tremendous interest in German poetry and folklore. They are best known for their collections of German fairy tales and for producing the *German Dictionary*, a pioneer effort that served as a model for later lexicographers. The first volume of *Grimm's Fairy Tales* (1812) contained eighty-six stories; the second, published in 1815, contained seventy.

A handsome volume to share with children of all ages is *Grimm's Fairy Tales* (Follett, 1968), a text based on the Frances Jenkins Olcott edition and illustrated with fifty paintings by children of fifteen nations. In this treasure chest you will find the popular stories "Little Red Riding Hood," "Hansel and Gretel," and "Sleeping Beauty" as well as many lesser known tales. Showing your children the paintings created by other girls and boys might inspire them to illustrate their own favorite Grimm character.

Single editions of the Grimm stories abound in library collections. Four for the younger set are the 1973 Caldecott Honor Book *Snow-White and the Seven Dwarfs* (Farrar, Straus, 1972) lavishly illustrated in full-color paintings by Nancy Ekholm Burkert, *Little Red Riding Hood* illustrated by Bernadette (World, 1968; also in paper, Scholastic Book Services), *Red Riding Hood* deliciously retold in verse by Beatrice Schenk de Regniers with droll illustrations by Edward Gorey (Atheneum, 1972), and *King Grisly-Beard*, translated by Edgar Taylor with illustrations by Maurice Sendak (Farrar, Straus, 1973). For teacher reference and for older readers the two-volume set entitled *The Juniper Tree and Other Tales from Grimm* selected by Lore Segal and Maurice Sendak with pictures by Maurice Sendak (Farrar, Straus, 1973) is not to be missed. Together they contain twenty-seven stories.

JANUARY 4, 1809
Birth Date of Louis Braille

Louis Braille was born in a village near Paris, France. At the age of three, while playing in his father's workshop, an awl pierced his eye, and he soon became totally blind. Seventeen years later he published a system of printing and writing for the blind, which he had adapted from the night writing system used by Charles Barbier, a French army captain. Soldiers sent messages at night by punching coded dots on thick paper. The Braille system employs raised dots representing letters, signs, and numbers. It is still used by blind people.

Middle-grade readers will enjoy *Louis Braille: The Boy Who Invented Books for the Blind* by Margaret Davidson (Scholastic Book Services, 1971).

JANUARY 4, 1885

The first appendectomy was performed in Davenport, Iowa, by Dr. William West Grant on patient Mary Gartside. How many of your students have had an appendectomy? Encourage them to discuss their experience. For younger children the book, *Let's Find Out About Hospitals* (Watts, 1972) by Eleanor Kay, a registered nurse, will help them understand that hospitals are not places to fear but places in which to get well quickly.

JANUARY 4, 1896

Utah became the forty-fifth state.

JANUARY 5, 1864
Birth Date of George Washington Carver

George Washington Carver, born a slave in Missouri, became one of America's leading scientists. In his experiments with the peanut he found more than three hundred products that could be made from it, including wood dyes, soap, linoleum, plastic, flour, paint, ink, and many different types of oil. Dr. Carver worked to bolster the economy and agriculture of the South by introducing new by-products for sweet potatoes, soybeans, and cotton stalks as well as the peanut.

After his death in 1943, many of his personal belongings and scientific papers were housed in the Carver Museum on the campus of Tuskegee Institute in Alabama where he had served as director of agricultural research for many years. In New York State today is celebrated as Carver Day.

An interesting story is told of how the name of America's first president became part of Carver's name. While he was in college another George Carver there often received his mail. He decided to add a middle name—Washington!

A fine book about Carver is *A Weed Is a Flower: The Life of George Washington Carver* written and illustrated by Aliki (Prentice-Hall). Although it is a picture book, all children in the elementary grades should enjoy it.

JANUARY 5, 1925

Nellie Taylor Ross became the first woman governor of a state—Wyoming. Do your children know who is the governor of their state?

JANUARY 6, 1878
Birth Date of Carl Sandburg

> If poems could be explained, then poets would
> have to leave out roses, sunsets, faces from their
> poems.*

Carl Sandburg, the son of Swedish immigrants, was born in Galesburg, Illinois. His birthplace at 331 East 3rd Street is now a memorial that attracts over 15,000 adult and child visitors each year. During his eighty-nine years Sandburg worked at a potpourri of jobs including journalist, political

---

* From the Preface, "Short Talk on Poetry" in *Early Moon*. New York: Harcourt, 1930.

organizer, historian, and singer of folk songs. Thirty years were spent researching and writing a six-volume biography of Abraham Lincoln; in 1940 he was awarded the Pulitzer Prize in History for the last four volumes, *Abraham Lincoln: The War Years* (Harcourt, 1939). In 1950 he received a second Pulitzer Prize, this time for *Complete Poems* (Harcourt, 1949).

Mr. Sandburg wrote two books of poetry for children, *Early Moon* (Harcourt, 1930) and *Wind Song* (Harcourt, 1960). The best volume to use with children in the elementary grades is *The Carl Sandburg Treasury: Prose and Poetry for Young People* (Harcourt, 1970), which includes the complete texts of both *Early Moon* and *Wind Song* as well as his famous *Rootabaga Stories, Abraham Lincoln Grows Up,* and *Prairie Town Boy.* Upper-grade students will enjoy *Carl Sandburg: Voice of the People* by Ruth Franchere (Garrard, 1970). Mature readers can handle *Carl Sandburg, Yes* by W. G. Rogers (Harcourt, 1970). All children can hear the poet read from his work on the recordings *Poems for Children* and *Carl Sandburg Reading Fog and Other Poems* (Caedmon, distributed by D. C. Heath).

JANUARY 6, 1912

New Mexico became the forty-seventh state.

JANUARY 7, 1800
Birth Date of Millard Fillmore

Thirteenth President

Born in:	Summer Hill, New York
Occupation:	Farmer, lawyer
President:	1850–1853, Whig
Died:	March 8, 1874
	Buffalo, New York

About Fillmore

🏴 Youth spent in poverty.

🏴 Enacted a law against debtors' prisons, jails for those who owed money.

🏴 Became president upon Zachary Taylor's death, July 9, 1850.

During His Term

🏴 Compromise of 1850 passed with the help of Daniel Webster and Henry Clay. It provided a ten-year respite in the North-South clash over slavery.

🏴 Created first White House library by bringing books into the executive mansion.

🏴 Dispatched Commodore Matthew Perry's fleet to Japan in 1853, opening up that nation to trade and diplomatic relations.

🏴 Approved the Fugitive Slave Bill.

JANUARY 9, 1788

Connecticut became the fifth state to ratify the Constitution.

JANUARY 9, 1913
Birth Date of Richard Milhous Nixon

Thirty-seventh President

      Born in: Yorba Linda, California
      Occupation: Congressman, senator, lawyer
      President: 1969–1974, Republican

About Nixon

🏴 Early anti-communist; leading member of House Committee on Un-American Activities.

🏴 Twice Eisenhower's vice-president.

🏴 Lost 1960 presidential election to Kennedy.

[79]

During His Terms

📰 Elected in 1968 and 1972 with Vice-president Spiro T. Agnew.

📰 Reelected to second term by landslide majority.

📰 Vice-president Agnew forced to resign because of criminal charges.

📰 Gerald R. Ford chosen vice-president in October 1973.

📰 Initiated progress in foreign affairs: Communist China admitted to the United Nations, detente with U.S.S.R. began, diplomatic relations with China reestablished, American troops withdrawn from Viet Nam, Henry Kissinger endeavored to mediate Middle Eastern peace.

📰 Resigned rather than face certain impeachment for Watergate scandal of June 17, 1972, and other abuses of presidential power.

JANUARY 11, 1878

A milkman in Brooklyn, New York, delivered milk in glass bottles to his customers for the first time. Encourage children to find out how milk was delivered prior to this. How is it delivered today? What are the advantages of cardboard containers over glass bottles? What are the disadvantages?

JANUARY 12, 1628
Birth Date of Charles Perrault

Fairy tales such as "Sleeping Beauty," "Little Red Riding Hood," "Cinderella," and "Puss in Boots" have been around for hundreds of years. These were tales that were passed down for generations by word of mouth. But it was either Charles Perrault, a member of the French Academy, or his eldest son, Pierre Perrault d'Armancour, who first wrote them down, preserving them for generations to come. In 1697 *Contes de Ma Mere l'Oye* (*Tales of Mother Goose*) was published; in 1729 it was translated into English.

There have been countless retellings of these tales; in the future there will undoubtedly be many more. Today is a good day to share one of the stories with a group of children. Younger boys and girls will enjoy listening to one. Older children might make comparisons of the tales. This is a particularly good activity for slower readers, for they can do a project without losing face. For example, they might compare both text and illustrations of Marcia Brown's Caldecott Award winning book, *Cinderella, or The Little Glass Slipper* (Scribner, 1954) with a later version of *Cinderella* by Nola Langer (Scholastic Book Services, paper, 1972). Better students might try their hand at writing parodies of the tales set in contemporary time. Some possibilities are: Cinderella Moves Next Door, Sleeping Beauty Wakes Up Today, Little Red Riding Hood Retells Her Story to Her Own Grandchildren. Another reading-writing project is to have children rewrite the tales or provide new endings to favorite versions.

JANUARY 12, 1737
Birth Date of John Hancock

"There! King George can read that without his spectacles," declared John Hancock in 1776 when he became the first man to sign the Declaration of Independence. He wrote his name on the document in large bold letters. Hancock, a Boston merchant, was an early advocate of independence. He served as president of the Continental Congress and was an outstanding rebel. To this day a signature is often referred to as a "John Hancock."

JANUARY 12, 1812

The first steamboat chugged down the Mississippi River to New Orleans. The Mississippi River, the longest in the United States, is sometimes called "Father of Waters." It flows for about 2,350 miles from near the Canadian border to the Gulf of Mexico. Hernando de Soto discovered the Mississippi in 1541, and it was explored in the 1670s by the Frenchman, Robert La Salle.

The score to the musical comedy *Show Boat* includes the famous song "Ol' Man River" composed by Jerome Kern. The class could sing the song or listen to a recording of it. Youngsters will enjoy *Little Toot on the Mississippi* by Hardie Gramatky (Putnam, 1973). Older boys and girls might compare the length of a river in their home or nearby state with the Mississippi.

JANUARY 14, 1875
Birth Date of Albert Schweitzer

Schweitzer was one of those rare geniuses who was involved in a multitude of activities. He was a theologian, philosopher, writer, medical doctor, an organist acclaimed for his interpretations of Johann Sebastian Bach's works, and a mission director in equatorial Africa. In 1899 he received a doctoral degree in philosophy; in 1900 another for theology, and in 1913 an M.D. degree. After receiving the latter, he and his wife Hélenè ventured to Lambaréné in Gabon province of French Africa where, with the help of natives, he built a hospital. Later he established a leper colony. In 1952 he was awarded the Nobel Peace Prize for his efforts in behalf of "The Brotherhood of Nations." Schweitzer died at Lambaréné at age ninety.

A fine biography for mature readers is *The Story of Albert Schweitzer* by Jo Manton (Abelard, 1955).

JANUARY 15, 1929
Birth Date of Martin Luther King, Jr.

Martin Lewis King, Jr. was born in Atlanta, Georgia. When he grew up he changed his middle name to Luther in honor of the Protestant leader, Martin Luther. After graduating from Morehouse College, Dr. King entered the ministry. He received many awards for his nonviolent, direct-action approach in seeking equal civil rights for all Americans. *Time* magazine chose him Man of the Year in 1963 for his leadership in the protests against segregation in Birmingham, Alabama. On August 28, 1963, Dr. King addressed more than 200,000 Americans who gathered at a march in Washington, D. C., to protest racial inequality in the United States. It was there that he made his famous "I Have a Dream" speech (see August 28). The following year he became the second black American to receive the Nobel Peace Prize. On April 4, 1968, Dr. King was assassinated in Memphis, Tennessee, while fighting for the rights of that city's sanitation workers. The United States observed a national mourning period of six days in memory of this great civil rights leader.

The following children's books will help students to understand the important role Dr. King played in contemporary history. For younger readers suggest *The Picture Life of Martin Luther King, Jr.* by Margaret B. Young (Watts, 1968). Older readers can try *The Life and Words of Martin Luther King, Jr.* by Ira Peck (Scholastic Book Services, paper, 1968; also available in book/record combination, *Martin Luther King, Jr.: A Musical Documentary*) and *An Album of Martin Luther King, Jr.* by Jeanne A. Rowe (Watts, 1970). Everyone will enjoy *I Am a Man: Ode to Martin Luther King, Jr.* by Eve Merriam (Doubleday, 1971).

[83]

JANUARY 17, 1706
Birth Date of Benjamin Franklin

Benjamin Franklin was the fifteenth child and youngest son in a Boston family of seventeen children. His parents were shop owners who made soap and candles. Young Franklin attended school for two years, where he was excellent in reading, fair in writing, and poor in arithmetic. At age ten he left school to help in his parents' shop. Learning on his own, Franklin became a jack-of-all-trades and master of many! As a publisher, he developed the *Pennsylvania Gazette* into one of the most successful newspapers in the colonies from 1729 to 1766; from 1733 to 1758 he both wrote and published *Poor Richard's Almanac,* which contained his wise and witty sayings such as "Early to bed and early to rise, makes a man healthy, wealthy and wise." He was also a civic leader, serving as Philadelphia's postmaster in 1737 and deputy postmaster general for all the colonies in 1753.

Throughout his life he displayed inventive talent. He was one of the first men in the world to experiment with electricity and invented the lightning rod (see June 15, 1752), the Franklin stove, and bifocal eyeglasses. He was also the first scientist to study the movement of the Gulf Stream in the Atlantic Ocean. Besides all this, Franklin established an academy in Philadelphia that became the University of Pennsylvania. Franklin's political efforts centered around the then evolving United States. He was one of the guiding hands in drawing up the Declaration of Independence and played an important role in the nation's formative years. He died on April 17, 1790, at the age of eighty-four.

There are several easy-to-read biographies available for younger readers. These include: *Benjamin Franklin* by Charles P. Graves (Garrard, 1960), *The Story of Ben*

Franklin by Eve Merriam (Four Winds Press, 1965; Scholastic Book Services, paper), and *Meet Benjamin Franklin* by Maggi Scarf (Random House, 1968). Middle-grade readers can learn about the many facets of Franklin's career—from printer to ambassador—in Jeanette Eaton's *That Lively Man: Benjamin Franklin* (Morrow, 1948). All children will enjoy reading or hearing selected parts of Robert Lawson's fictionalized biography, *Ben and Me* (Little, Brown, 1939, 1959; Dell, paper), a tale about the man as told by his good friend, Amos the mouse, who lived in Franklin's fur cap.

JANUARY 17, 1942
Birth Date of Muhammed Ali (Cassius Clay)

Muhammed Ali, born Cassius Marcellus Clay in Louisville, Kentucky, was taught to box by a policeman, Joe Martin. When he was seventeen, he won the national Golden Gloves light heavyweight championship. The next year in Rome, Italy, he was acclaimed the amateur light heavyweight champion of the world. Ali's style, colorful statements such as "I'm the greatest!" and his writing of poetry made him a natural crowd builder and one who revitalized the boxing world. When he turned professional, he became the heavyweight champion of the world when he defeated Sonny Liston.

The name Muhammed Ali was given him by Elijah Muhammed, leader of the Nation of Islam, a deeply religious group of Black Muslims. Ali lost his heavyweight title in 1967 when he refused to enter the armed forces; the Supreme Court later upheld his right to refuse induction because of his religious convictions. In 1971 he was defeated by Joe Frazier, who became the new world heavyweight champion. In 1974 he won his title back from

George Foreman in a match held in Zaire, Africa, becoming the second heavyweight in history to regain the crown. On December 9, 1974, New York City honored the champ by celebrating Muhammed Ali Day when he was given the city's Bronze Medallion.

An easy-to-read biography is *Muhammed Ali* by Beth P. Wilson (Putnam, 1974.)

JANUARY 18, 1882
Birth Date of A. A. Milne

For nearly forty-five years children and adults have selected *Winnie-the-Pooh* stories from library shelves and have taken them into their homes and hearts. Younger children love to hear the stories read aloud; older girls and boys reread them; college students study the whimsy of Pooh's adventures along with the writings of Shakespeare and Salinger.

The author of the Pooh stories was London-born Alan Alexander Milne who died on January 31, 1956. His first book for children, *When We Were Very Young* (Dutton, 1924), is his classic collection of poems written for his three-year-old son, Christopher Robin. This was followed by *Now We Are Six* (Dutton, 1927). *Winnie-the-Pooh* (Dutton, 1926) and *The House at Pooh Corner* (Dutton, 1928; both in paper) are stories about Milne's son's stuffed animals. Illustrated by Ernest Shepard, they have become the most successful books ever created for children.

There are countless editions of Milne's work available in hardcover and paperback volumes as well as The-World-of-Pooh dolls, toys, calendars, and films. Although aimed at adult audiences, the film *Mr. Shepard and Mr. Milne* (Weston Woods) will interest children in the upper grades who are young enough to recall the books and old enough to be fascinated with the people who created them. Share some of Milne's stories and verse with younger boys and girls—they will love them. A group of middle-grade youngsters might enjoy reading and/or rereading some of Milne's work, planning a dramatized version of several poems or a chapter from the Pooh books and presenting it as an assembly program or entertainment for lower-grade classes.

JANUARY 19, 1807
Birth Date of Robert Edward Lee

"Who does not love General Lee, who would not barter life for his smile?"

The above quotation was written by a Confederate foot soldier during the Gettysburg campaign. In just one sentence it tells how much General Robert E. Lee was loved. Lee commanded the largest Confederate field force, the Army of Northern Virginia, during most of the Civil War. His leadership earned him a place in history as one of the world's greatest military commanders.

A native Virginian, he graduated from West Point, ranking first in his class. Years later he was superintendent of West Point. Lee fought with valor in the Mexican War and was offered the command of the Union army by President Lincoln on the eve of the Civil War. In 1859, he led the detachment of United States troops that captured John Brown and his anti-slavery raiders at Harpers Ferry, Virginia (see May 9). He did not believe in slavery or breaking up the Union, but when the Civil War came, he felt greater loyalty to Virginia than to the Union.

After organizing and training Virginia's forces, he took over the command of all the Confederate armies. Although he won many important victories, the tide began to turn in

1863; he lost his ablest general, Stonewall Jackson, at Chancellorsville and suffered defeat at the Battle of Gettysburg (see July 1). In April 1865, after a long and bitter retreat though Virginia, he surrendered to General Ulysses S. Grant at the Appomattox courthouse, ending the War between the States.

After the Civil War, General Lee urged the North and South to reconcile their differences. In the years since, he has been admired in the North as well as the South. In 1900 he was elected to the Hall of Fame. His estate is now Arlington National Cemetery, and the Curtis-Lee Mansion that overlooks the cemetery is a national monument. In many Southern states today is a legal holiday to honor Lee.

Three easy-to-read biographies of Lee for middle-graders are: *Robert E. Lee: Hero of the South* by Charles P. Graves (Garrard, 1964), *Robert E. Lee: Soldier of the South* by Jean Rikhoff (Putnam, 1968), and *Meet Robert E. Lee* by George Swift Trow (Random House, 1969).

JANUARY 20
Presidential Inauguration Day

Every four years on this date a president of the United States is inaugurated. Until 1933 American presidents took their oath of office on March 4. When the Twentieth Amendment was passed, January 20 became the official date for office taking. President James Monroe was first to take the oath and deliver his address at the Capitol Building in Washington, D. C. James Madison gave the first inaugural ball, a formal reception and celebration that is now part of today's tradition.

JANUARY 21

The zodiac sign, Aquarius the Water Bearer, begins today and ends on February 19. How many children in the class were born under this sign?

JANUARY 21, 1832
Birth Date of Lewis Carroll

Lewis Carroll's real name was Charles Lutwidge Dodgson, and he was a teacher of mathematics at Oxford University. He used the pen name Lewis Carroll when he published his classics, *Alice's Adventures in Wonderland* and *Through the Looking Glass*. The adventures of Alice evolved from his telling stories to a real Alice, Alice Liddell, a daughter of a devoted friend. One Christmas he wrote and illustrated the story as a gift to her. (Years later the original manuscript of ninety-two pages was sold to a private collector in the United States for £15,400 or about $77,000!) Several years later, the story was issued in book form with Sir John Tenniel's famed illustrations; today such characters as White Rabbit, the Cheshire Cat, and the Mad Hatter are as fresh as when they first appeared.

Unfortunately, many middle-grade children are turned off by the full-length book because it seems "babyish." The novel is certainly a great one for some fifth- and sixth-graders; it is filled with adventure, rhyme, and fantasy—all the elements that appeal to ten, eleven, and twelve year olds (and beyond!). One of the reasons some children do not read the book is because it has been abridged in countless editions, including the Walt Disney film version.

Boys and girls will enjoy hearing selected chapters and/or several of the nonsense rhymes such as "Beautiful Soup," the January poem of the month. Encourage several upper-grade children to read the complete Alice books and report on them to the entire class. This might interest others. A paperback edition of *Alice in Wonderland*, with Sir John Tenniel's original illustrations, is available from Scholastic Book Services. *Poems of Lewis Carroll* selected by Myra Cohn Livingston (T. Y. Crowell, 1973) features a bounty of his work and contains illustrations by many artists in other editions of Carroll's books.

JANUARY 24, 1848

John Sutter found gold near his mill in the Sacramento Valley, California. His discovery attracted thousands of people to the area near San Francisco in what was known as the Gold Rush of 1848. Man has always sought this scarce metal. Primitive peoples used it for jewelry and artwork. Modern nations have used it to back up paper currency; today it is in such short supply that this practice has been abandoned. Students can observe the anniversary of Sutter's discovery by reporting on the importance of gold in societies past and present.

JANUARY 24, 1925
Birth Date of Maria Tallchief

Maria Tallchief is an American ballerina who has been internationally praised for her graceful dancing. She is one of the first American ballerinas to gain international fame and prove that American ballet can equal the quality of European dancing. In 1942 Ms. Tallchief made her debut with the Ballet Russe de Monte Carlo and five years later joined the New York City Ballet—the year the corps was founded. She was born in Oklahoma, the daughter of an Osage Indian father and Scotch-Irish mother.

[90]

Two fine, easy-to-read biographies are *Maria Tallchief* by Tobi Tobias (T. Y. Crowell, 1970) and *Maria Tallchief: American Ballerina* Adele DeLeeuw (Garrard, 1971). Children interested in the ballet will also enjoy *The First Book of the Ballet* by Noel Streatfield (Watts, 1953) and *The Royal Book of the Ballet* by Shirley Goulden (Follett, 1973).

JANUARY 26, 1788

The world's only country-continent, Australia, was first settled by colonists who were convicts transported from England. Known for its great coral reef, kangaroos, and eucalyptus trees, the largest island on earth is an interesting place for children to study. The nineteenth century Australian folk song "Waltzing Matilda" became a World War II favorite. Boys and girls will enjoy singing or listening to this catchy tune as part of their Australian experience.

JANUARY 26, 1837

Michigan became the twenty-sixth state.

JANUARY 27, 1756
Birth Date of Wolfgang Amadeus Mozart

Austrian-born Mozart began his musical career by playing the harpsichord at the age of three. By the time he was six he had learned to play the violin and organ and could compose music of his own. He gave his first public performance when he was only five, and he and his older sister played throughout Germany, France, and England for kings, queens, and other nobility. Needless to say, people everywhere were astounded at this musical prodigy. When he became thirteen, his father took him to Italy where he wrote all kinds of music and was honored by other musicians and audiences everywhere he played. Unfortunately his later years were not as happy as his youth. He became quite poor, died early at age thirty-five, and was buried in an unmarked pauper's grave. During his lifetime he created more than six hundred works of music —forty-one symphonies, many concertos, masses, church music, quartets, and twenty famous operas including *The Magic Flute, The Marriage of Figaro,* and *Don Giovanni.*

Upper-grade students can learn more about this remarkable musician in *Mozart* by Manuel Komroff (Knopf, 1956), a biography written to commemorate the two hundredth anniversary of his birth.

JANUARY 29, 1843
Birth Date of William McKinley

Twenty-fifth President

Born in:	Niles, Ohio
Occupation:	Lawyer, congressman
President:	1897–1901, Republican
Died:	September 14, 1901
	Buffalo, New York
	Buried in Canton, Ohio

About McKinley

▨ Working class background; son of a foundryman.

▨ Served in the Civil War as a private, rising to the rank of major under his friend General Rutherford B. Hayes, who became the nineteenth president.

▨ Advocate of tariffs.

▨ Governor of Ohio.

▨ Campaigns made use of telephone for the first time.

During His Term

🏴 U.S. Battleship *Maine* blown up in Havana Harbor, setting off the Spanish-American War.

🏴 Assassinated by an anarchist on September 6, 1901, while visiting the Pan-American Exposition in Buffalo, New York.

🏴 Acquired the Philippine Islands from Spain and annexed Hawaii.

JANUARY 29, 1861

Kansas became the thirty-fourth state.

JANUARY 30, 1882
Birth Date of Franklin Delano Roosevelt

Thirty-second President

Born in:	Hyde Park, New York
Occupation:	Public official, lawyer
President:	1933–1945, Democrat
Died:	April 12, 1945
	Warm Springs, Georgia
	Buried in Hyde Park, New York

About Roosevelt

🏴 An only child.

🏴 Crippled by polio in 1921, he thereafter wore leg braces.

🏴 Woodrow Wilson's Assistant Secretary of the Navy and later governor of New York.

During His Term

🏴 Helped nation survive Depression with the "alphabet soup" agencies of the New Deal and his optimistic spirit.

[93]

■ Appointed first woman cabinet member—Frances Perkins, Secretary of Labor.

■ First president to seek more than two terms of office; he was elected four times.

■ His wife Eleanor became a world famous leader and humanitarian.

■ Under his leadership the United States became a world power. He encouraged the creation of the United Nations, which was organized at the end of World War II.

■ Died in office.

JANUARY 31, 1797
Birth Date of Franz Peter Schubert

Franz Schubert can be introduced to students via the picture book *A Little Schubert* by M. B. Goffstein (Harper, 1972). The simple text offers a brief glimpse of the composer in his later life. Included with it is a 7-inch LP recording of five of the twelve "Noble Waltzes" Schubert composed in his little room in Vienna, played on the piano by Peter Schaaf, the author's husband. Born in Vienna, Austria, Franz Schubert was one of a large music-loving family. He received his music education from his father and elder brothers early in life. He played the piano as soon as he was big enough to reach the keys and composed tunes as soon as he could write notes. During his short life he produced over 600 art songs, or *lieder*, sometimes as many as eight a day. Besides *lieder*, he wrote music for the orchestra, chorus, chamber groups, and piano. His *Eighth Symphony*, also called *The Unfinished*, is one of his finest orchestral works. Despite his productivity as a composer, Schubert received very little recognition during his lifetime and was never able to earn an income sufficient to support himself.

In 1822 Schubert made the acquaintance of Ludwig van Beethoven, who later acclaimed his work. Schubert was elected to the Musical Society of Vienna and despite ill health managed to give his first public concert, which was a great success. Publishers began to request his work, and his future seemed assured—but it was too late. On November 19, 1828, Schubert died at the age of thirty-one.

JANUARY/FEBRUARY
Chinese New Year

Orientals begin their New Year festivities in late January and early February. The event takes place with the first new moon after the sun enters Aquarius and is celebrated for fifteen days. Each new year is named for one of twelve animals: the mouse, ox, tiger, rabbit, dragon, snake, horse, sheep, monkey, rooster, dog, or boar. People spend the day visiting relatives and friends. Many bring a traditional gift of fruit and red paper envelopes containing li shee (money) for the children; these are considered lucky both to give and receive. Traditional New Year parades are led by the Golden Dragon, the Chinese symbol of strength.

Share the picture book, which can be enjoyed by all children, *Twelve Years, Twelve Animals* (Abingdon, 1972), a Japanese folktale adopted by Yoshiko Samuel. It explains how the years received their various animal names. Another book to share is the Caldecott Award winning volume, *Mei Li* by Thomas Handforth (Doubleday, 1938). The story is about a young girl who goes with her brother to the New Year's Day fair in Peking from their home in North China.

FEBRUARY

Flower—Violet   Birthstone—Amethyst

The second month's name is derived from the Latin word *Februarius*, which in turn stems from the verb *februare* meaning to *expiate* or *purify*. To the Romans February was the "month of purification" when people repented their wrongdoings and offered sacrifices to the gods.

The month was not included in the original Roman calendar, which had only ten months. About 700 B.C. Numo Pompilius, Rome's second king, added two new months; he assigned January to begin the year and February to end it. February became the second month in 452 B.C. Augustus Caesar, a later emperor of Rome, made February the shortest month when he took a day from its twenty-nine to make the month bearing his name, August, longer. He did this so that his month would have as many days as July, named for his uncle, Julius Caesar.

[97]

POEM OF THE MONTH

DREAMS

Hold fast to dreams
For if dreams die
Life is a broken-winged bird
That cannot fly.

Hold fast to dreams
For when dreams go
Life is a barren field
Frozen with snow.

—Langston Hughes

FEBRUARY 1, 1902
Birth Date of Langston Hughes

> For a whole race of people freed from slavery
> without nothing—without money, without work,
> without education—it has not always been easy
> to hold fast to dreams. But the Negro people be-
> lieved in the American dream. Now, since almost
> a hundred years of freedom, we've come a long
> way. But there is still a way for the Negro—and
> democracy to go.*

Langston Hughes was born in Joplin, Missouri. During
his childhood, he moved from one place to another, from
relative to relative. A perfect way to begin February, or any
month, is to share with children the beautiful words of
this great poet. The February poem of the month,

* From text of the recording *The Dream Keeper and Other Poems*
(Folkways Records).

"Dreams," conveys a beautiful message to any aged child.

Hughes' life is detailed in several biographies for young readers including *Langston Hughes: A Biography* by Milton Meltzer (T. Y. Crowell, 1968), *Langston Hughes: Poet of His People* by Elisabeth M. Myers (Garrard, 1970), *Black Troubador: Langston Hughes* by Charlemae Hill Rollins (Rand McNally, 1970), and *Langston Hughes: American Poet* by Alice Walker (T. Y. Crowell, 1974). For teachers, an excellent study of Langston Hughes' work appears in *Black Poets of the United States* by Jean Wagner (University of Illinois Press, 1973; also in paper).

Hughes's first published poem, "The Negro Speaks of Rivers," appeared in 1919 in *The Crisis*, the official magazine of the National Association for the Advancement of Colored People. From that date on until his death on May 27, 1967, his work was widely published. Besides poetry he wrote plays, nonfiction books for children and adults, novels, short stories, operettas, and newspaper columns. It was his poetry, however, that earned him the title of Black Poet Laureate. Children can hear Langston Hughes talk about his life and read his poetry on the recording *The Dream Keeper and Other Poems* (Folkways). Forty-five of his poems for children appear in *Don't You Turn Back: Poems by Langston Hughes* selected by Lee Bennett Hopkins (Knopf, 1969).

FEBRUARY 2
Groundhog Day

According to a German legend passed on from the Middle Ages, the groundhog is said to come out of hibernation on this day. If it sees its shadow because the skies are sunny, it will return to its burrow beneath the ground for another six weeks of winter sleep. If it does not see its shadow because the skies are overcast, winter will be shorter, and an earlier spring will come. Have someone in the class check the newspaper tonight to see what happened to the groundhog's shadow.

FEBRUARY 3, 1821
Birth Date of Elizabeth Blackwell

Elizabeth Blackwell, the first American woman doctor, was granted her medical degree from Geneva Medical School in Geneva, New York, in 1849. Born in Bristol, England, her family came to the United States in 1832. After her father's death, she taught school for several years to help support her family. In 1844 she decided to become a physician but was refused admittance to medical schools in Philadelphia and New York City. For three years she studied privately, until she gained entrance to Geneva Medical School. In 1853 she opened a dispensary in New York City staffed entirely by women; this later became the New York Infirmary. After the Civil War she founded the Women's Medical College, associated with the Infirmary.

There is a long poem suited to middle-graders about the doctor in *Independent Voices* by Eve Merriam (Atheneum, 1968). A short but informative biographical account of her life appears in *Women Who Shaped History* by Henrietta Buckmaster (Collier/Macmillan, paper, 1974).

FEBRUARY 6, 1788

Massachusetts was the sixth state to ratify the Constitution.

[100]

FEBRUARY 7, 1812
Birth Date of Charles Dickens

Charles Dickens was born in Portsmouth, England. A bright youngster, he learned to read and write at an early age, but when he was only eleven years old, his education was arrested because his father was imprisoned for being in debt. Young Dickens had to work in a factory to help support his family. The cruel treatment and harsh living conditions he endured were vividly remembered and are recreated in his writings. Later when his father inherited some money, he was sent to a boarding school. In his late teens he became a newspaper reporter in Parliament and soon rose to the top of his profession.

His fame as a writer began with the publication of *Pickwick Papers* (1837) and continued with such works as *A Tale of Two Cities, Oliver Twist, David Copperfield,* and *Great Expectations,* many of which are thought to contain incidents based on his early life experiences. *A Christmas Carol,* featuring the greatest people-hater of all times—Scrooge—has become one of the favorite and best-loved Christmas stories.

Dickens was the father of ten children. He supplemented his writing income by giving a series of popular lecture tours and on two occasions visited the United States and read to audiences.

FEBRUARY 7, 1867
Birth Date of Laura Ingalls Wilder

Laura Ingalls Wilder authored the popular "Little House" books—pioneer stories for middle-grade readers based on her own life growing up on the late nineteenth century American frontier. She began to write the series when she was sixty-five. The first, *Little House in the Big Woods* (1932; all published by Harper and now in paperback editions), was followed by *Farmer Boy* (1933), the story of her husband's boyhood in northern New York State, *Little House on the Prairie* (1935), *On the Banks of Plum Creek* (1937), *By the Shores of Silver Lake* (1939), *The Long Winter* (1940), *Little Town on the Prairie* (1941), and *These Happy Golden Years* (1943). Ms. Wilder lived on her farm in Mansfield, Missouri, until her death, at the age of ninety. The manuscript for the ninth "Little House" book was discovered among her papers. Entitled *The First Four Years*, it was published in 1971, exactly as she wrote it. Although all of the stories in the series are written in the third person, they are told with humor and warmth and give readers a realistic account of American pioneer life. Her farm is now a museum that is visited every year by many children and adults.

In 1954 the Laura Ingalls Wilder Award for lasting contributions to children's literature was established by the American Library Association. Ms. Wilder received the first award, which is given every five years to an author or artist whose body of work is outstanding. A television series, "Little House on the Prairie," based on the books, has been produced. Of interest for both student and teacher reference are *West from Home: Letters of Laura Ingalls Wilder, San Francisco 1915* edited by Roger Lea MacBride (Harper, 1974), *On the Way Home: The Diary of a Trip from South Dakota to Mansfield, Missouri, in 1894* by Laura Ingalls Wilder (Harper, 1962), and *The Laura Ingalls Wilder Songbook: Favorite Songs from the "Little House" Books* compiled and edited by Eugenia Garson (Harper, 1968).

FEBRUARY 9, 1773
Birth Date of William Henry Harrison

Ninth President
> Born in: Charles County, Virginia
> Occupation: Soldier
> President: 1841, Whig
> Died: April 4, 1841
>   Washington, D.C.
>   Buried in North Bend, Ohio

About Harrison
> 🏴 Only president who studied to be a doctor—he never made it!
> 🏴 Negotiator and fighter of Indians. Defeated Tecumseh, Shawnee Chief, at Battle of Tippecanoe in 1811.

During His Term
> 🏴 Called "Granny" by Democrats because of his age, 68.
> 🏴 Died one month after taking office.

FEBRUARY 10, 1950
Birth Date of Mark Spitz

Born in Modesto, California, Mark Spitz began splashing in the Pacific Ocean off Honolulu, Hawaii, when he was two years old. By the time he was ten, he was swimming ninety minutes a day, seven days a week. At fourteen, he qualified for the United States Amateur Athletic Union (AAU) competition and won four gold medals the following year in Tel Aviv's Maccabiah Games. At the 1967 Pan-American Games he won five gold medals. Two years later he took six gold medals at Tel Aviv; in 1972 he won the AAU's Sullivan Award as the outstanding amateur athlete of 1971. Spitz set a world record at the 1972 Olympic Games in Munich by winning seven gold medals, the first athlete to win more than five gold medals in one Olympiad.

FEBRUARY 11, 1751

The first hospital in America opened in Philadelphia. The Pennsylvania Hospital was established with the assistance of Benjamin Franklin and Dr. Thomas Hood. It is still functioning. The word *hospital* comes from the Latin word *hospitium* meaning *house* or *institution for guests*.

FEBRUARY 11, 1847
Birth Date of Thomas Alva Edison

Thomas Alva Edison's inventions are all around us— the light bulb, phonograph, copying machine, storage battery, and ticker tape machine are just a few. From the time he grew up in Milan, Ohio, until he headed a great laboratory in Menlo Park, New Jersey, Edison was always tinkering. Despite having received only three months of formal education, the great inventor patented 1,100 devices in sixty years, which earned him the title "The Wizard of Menlo Park."

Beginning readers will enjoy *Thomas Alva Edison: Miracle Maker* by Mervyn D. Kaufman (Garrard, 1962). Older girls and boys can read *Young Thomas Edison* by Sterling North (Houghton, 1958).

FEBRUARY 12, 1809
Birth Date of Charles Darwin

Charles Darwin showed an interest in natural history at an early age. His father was a distinguished physician as was his grandfather. Charles also trained to be a physician but disliked it. With the idea of preparing for service in the church, he transferred to Cambridge University and graduated in 1831. In December of that year, he obtained a position as a naturalist on the ship *Beagle* and sailed on a scientific cruise around the world for five years. One of the most significant stops was the Galapagos Islands, an archipelago of volcanic rock some six hundred miles off the Pacific coast of Ecuador. Darwin noted the unique nature of the reptiles, plants, and fish native to this isolated site. He studied thousands of specimens of animal and plant life and developed a new concept of evolution, which gave him much of the material for his first book, *The Origin of Species*, published in 1859. The entire first edition of 1,250 copies sold out the first day it appeared. Darwin's theory of evolution caused great debate in England and all over the world. In 1871 he aroused more unfriendly criticism with his *The Descent of Man*. Although his theory is still debated, its fundamental principles prevail throughout the scientific world.

Children can locate the Galapagos Islands on a world map. A group might report how geographical isolation arrested the development of the species living there.

FEBRUARY 12, 1809
Birth Date of Abraham Lincoln

Sixteenth President

Born in: Hardin County, Kentucky
Occupation: Lawyer
President: 1861–1865, Republican
Died: April 15, 1865
Washington, D.C.
Buried in Springfield, Illinois

About Lincoln

▨ Frontier background in Kentucky, Indiana, and Illinois.

▨ Grew his beard at the request of an eleven-year-old supporter, Grace Bedell, who felt it would help his image.

[105]

🏴 Unsuccessful in his bid for Senate seat from Illinois. His 1858 debates with Stephen A. Douglas, a Democrat, made him famous.

During His Terms
🏴 Eleven Southern states seceded from the Union.
🏴 Civil War began when Confederate troops fired on Fort Sumter.
🏴 He directed Union army at first because of lack of trustworthy general.
🏴 Emancipation Proclamation issued (see January 1, 1863).
🏴 General Lee and his army surrendered April 9, 1865.
🏴 Assassinated on April 14, 1865, at Ford's Theatre, Washington, D. C., after starting second term.

FEBRUARY
Black History Week

The week that includes both the dates of Abraham Lincoln's birth and Frederick Douglass' death is celebrated as Black History Week. It was initiated in 1926 by Carter G. Woodson, a black historian, and the Association of the Study of Negro Life and History in Washington, D. C.

You might tie poetry into the celebration of Black History Week by using some poems by Langston Hughes (see poem of the month for February) or Gwendolyn Brooks (see poem of the month for June). Upper-grade children can read about important but little known roles played by blacks in the development of the United States. They can either report orally or plan a bulletin board display featuring black Americans and their contributions. An excellent bibliography, *The Black Experience in Chil-*

dren's Books compiled by Augusta Baker (New York Public Library, 1971, revised 1974) features a wide range of materials for all children.

FEBRUARY 12, 1846
Birth Date of Randolph Caldecott

Randolph Caldecott was born in Chester, England, and began drawing when a young boy. In 1871 several of his drawings appeared in the London magazine, *London Society*. The following year he settled in London to work as an artist. When Washington Irving's *Old Christmas* appeared with his illustrations in 1876, Caldecott's reputation was firmly established. Two years later he began working on nursery toy books. His most famous illustrations, however, were those for William Cowper's poem, *The Diverting History of John Gilpin*. In 1886 Caldecott made a trip to the United States, and during it he died in Florida.

The Caldecott Medal was named for this artist. This award, begun in 1938, is given annually by the American Library Association to the artist of the most distinguished picture book for children. The picture on the medal is taken from *The Diverting History of John Gilpin*.

Recent Caldecott Award books are:

1975 *Arrow to the Sun* illustrated by Gerald McDermott (Viking).

1974 *Duffy and the Devil* illustrated by Margot Zemach (Farrar, Straus).

1973 *The Funny Little Woman* illustrated by Blair Lent (Dutton).

1972 *One Fine Day* by Nonny Hogrogian (Macmillan).

1971 *A Story, A Story* illustrated by Gail E. Haley (Atheneum).

1970 *Sylvester and the Magic Pebble* illustrated and written by William Steig (Simon and Schuster).

Encourage children to seek out books that have received this prestigious award. Your school or public librarian can furnish a list of all of the winners from 1938 to the present. One group of children might report on the various techniques used to illustrate children's books (pen drawings, collage, watercolor, woodcuts, and so on). Upper-grade children might select some of the award-winning books to read and/or dramatize for lower-grade girls and boys.

FEBRUARY 14
Valentine's Day

The origins of Valentine's Day are unknown. Some historians say the celebration goes back to ancient Rome. William Shakespeare wrote about the day in the sixteenth century in *Hamlet*:

> Good morrow! 'Tis St. Valentine's Day
> All in the morning betime
> And I a maid at your window
> To be your valentine.

Most people believe that the day received its name from a man named Valentine who lived 1700 years ago. He was a priest in Rome when Christianity was a new religion, and he was put to death for teaching Christianity and later was named a saint.

Valentine greetings were popular as early as the Middle Ages when lovers usually said or sang their Valentine greetings to their sweethearts, since few could read or write. Written valentines began about the year 1400. The oldest one on record was made in 1415 by Charles, Duke of Orleans, a Frenchman who was captured by the English and imprisoned in the Tower of London. There he wrote valentine poems, some of which are in the British Museum.

In America Valentine's Day became popular through the efforts of Esther Howland whose father owned a store in Worcester, Massachusetts. After receiving a lacy valentine from England in 1847, she decided to make her own to sell in her father's shop. Demands for her original cards became so great that she started a business that earned her close to $100,000 a year.

Children will enjoy making their own valentines to send to family and friends. Why not post the phrase "I Love You" on a bulletin board in English and a variety of other languages? Here is the phrase in several languages:

		Pronunciation
French:	*Je t'aime*	Jeh TE-mm
Spanish:	*Yo te amo*	Yoh te A-moh
Italian:	*Io t'amo*	E-o tee-A-moh
German:	*Ich liebe dich*	eeksh LEE-beh deeksh
Hebrew:	*Ani ohev otach*	ah-NEE o-HEV O-tach
Japanese:	*Watakushi-wa anata-wo aishimasu*	WA-ta-SHE-wa an-A-ta-o ah-e-she-MA-sue

Young readers will enjoy the easy-to-read books *Valentine's Day* by Elizabeth Guilfoile (Garrard, 1965) and *St. Valentine's Day* by Clyde Robert Bulla (T. Y. Crowell, 1965). Older girls and boys will learn a great deal from *Hearts, Cupids, and Red Roses: The Story of the Valentine Symbols* by Edna Barth (Seabury, 1974). All ages will enjoy the anthology *Good Morning to You, Valentine* selected by Lee Bennett Hopkins (Harcourt, 1975).

FEBRUARY 14, 1859

Oregon became the thirty-third state.

FEBRUARY 14, 1912

Arizona became the forty-eighth state.

FEBRUARY 15, 1564
Birth Date of Galileo Galilei

Galileo was an Italian astronomer and physicist, whose contention that the earth moves around the sun generated enormous controversy when it was published. Galileo was punished and forced to recant his statement. He is remembered as a scientific genius for his work in astronomy, his discovery of four of Jupiter's moons, and his pioneering efforts in determining the speed of falling bodies. A biography for mature readers is *Galileo and the Magic Numbers* by Sidney Rosen (Little, Brown, 1958).

FEBRUARY 15, 1820
Birth Date of Susan B. Anthony

> I am a firm and full believer in the revelation that it is through woman that the race is to be redeemed.
>
> —from a speech by Susan B. Anthony

Susan B. Anthony was a reformer and leader in the American woman suffrage movement. Among the things she worked for were women's right to vote, women's property rights, higher wages for teachers, and the abolition of slavery. When the Fourteenth and Fifteenth Amendments to the Constitution were proposed to extend civil rights and grant the vote to male blacks, Ms. Anthony demanded that the provisions also apply to women. Failing to achieve this, she voted as a citizen and person but was arrested, tried, and fined. In 1869 she organized the Woman Suffrage Association and later the National American Woman Suffrage Association. Throughout the rest of her life she continued the struggle to attain women's rights, blazing the trail for the adoption of the Nineteenth Amendment (woman suffrage), which was finally ratified fourteen years after her death in 1906.

The many contributions of women throughout history can be found in the informative *An Album of Women in American History* by Claire R. and Leonard W. Ingraham (Watts, 1972). Have the class discuss women's liberation. Why not start by having the children tell what their mothers do for a living? This can serve as a jumping-off point to raise the consciousness of girls and boys as to what women's liberation truly means.

FEBRUARY 17, 1902
Birth Date of Marian Anderson

Marian Anderson was born in Philadelphia and began singing in choirs when she was six. At seventeen she was chosen from among three hundred contestants to sing with the New York Philharmonic Orchestra. Her first recital in Carnegie Hall in 1935 was an enormous success and was followed by many concert tours throughout the world. She was the first black to be employed as a member of the Metropolitan Opera Company in New York. In 1958 President Dwight D. Eisenhower appointed her to the United States Delegation to the United Nations.

Marian Anderson by Tobi Tobias (T. Y. Crowell, 1972) tells her life story to younger readers. Mature students can read all or parts of Ms. Anderson's biography, *My Lord, What a Morning* (Viking, 1956; also in paper from Avon).

[111]

FEBRUARY 18, 1930

While watching the heavens from an observatory in Arizona, Clyde Tombaugh, an astronomer, discovered Pluto, the outermost of the nine planets in our solar system. Pluto is smaller than earth, fifty times more distant from the sun, and has no moons. It can only be seen with the aid of powerful telescopes.

Encourage a group of children to construct a model of the solar system showing the relationship of the sun to the nine planets. Upper-graders will find it challenging to make scale models of each planet. This will reinforce their knowledge of the planets' relative sizes.

The positions of the planets outward from the sun are: Mercury, Venus, Earth, Mars, Jupiter, Saturn, Uranus, Neptune, and Pluto. Be sure to see September 23 and February 15, as well as tomorrow's date too. They are all astronomical!

FEBRUARY 19, 1473
Birth Date of Nicolaus Copernicus

Copernicus was an astronomer of Polish descent who founded modern astronomy around 1543 with his discovery that the earth is a moving planet and that the sun is the center of the solar system. Prior to this, astronomers accepted the geocentric (earth-center) theory of Ptolemy, an astronomer who lived about 100–170 A.D.

FEBRUARY 20

The zodiac sign, Pisces the Fish, begins today and ends on March 20. How many children in the class were born under this sign?

FEBRUARY 20, 1872

The Metropolitan Museum of Art opened in New York City. It is the largest art museum in the United States and contains more than one million items. Older girls and boys can "visit" the museum via the delightful Newbery Award winning book, *From the Mixed-Up Files of Mrs. Basil E. Frankweiler* by Elaine L. Konigsburg (Atheneum, 1968; also in paper). This is a story about two suburban children who run away from their Connecticut home and live hidden in the museum. Miller-Brody Productions, Inc. has recorded a dramatization of the book; it has also been made into a film starring Ingrid Bergman.

Sharing information about the museum might spark a visit to a local art museum. Perhaps the class can make their own museum corner where their paintings, drawings, and sculpture can be placed.

You can encourage interest in art by displaying reproductions of famous paintings. If they are not available through your school system, a good source is Giant Photos. This company offers reproductions of great masters' works for twenty–thirty cents each. Send for their illustrated catalog.

FEBRUARY 20, 1895
Death of Frederick Douglass

Frederick Augustus Washington Bailey, born a slave in Tuckahoe, Maryland, in 1817 (his actual birth date is unknown), was a journalist, statesman, and an important figure in the movement to abolish slavery in the United States. When he was twenty-one, he escaped from his master, changed his last name, and fled to New Bedford, Massachusetts. Shortly afterwards, Douglass lectured before anti-slavery societies in Massachusetts, Great Britain, and Ireland. On his return to the United States, he bought his freedom and founded and edited the *North Star,* a famous anti-slavery newspaper. At the beginning of the Civil War, he urged President Lincoln to recruit black soldiers. The first two black men to join the Northern army were Douglass' own sons.

Middle-grade children can learn more about the life and times of Douglass in Lillie Patterson's *Frederick Douglass: Freedom Fighter* (Garrard, 1965) and Margaret Davidson's *Frederick Douglass Fights for Freedom* (Four Winds Press, 1970; also in paper from Scholastic Book Services). A long poem about the man and his life appears in *Independent Voices* by Eve Merriam (Atheneum, 1968).

FEBRUARY 20, 1962

John Glenn became the first American astronaut to make a three-orbit flight in less than five hours aboard *Friendship 7.* Glenn is one of the most famous American airmen since Charles A. Lindbergh made the first solo flight across the Atlantic Ocean in 1927.

FEBRUARY 22, 1732
Birth Date of George Washington

First President

Born in:	Pope's Creek, Virginia
Occupation:	Planter, soldier
President:	1789–1797, Federalist
Died:	December 14, 1799
	Mount Vernon, Virginia

About Washington

▨ Soldier in the French and Indian War.

▨ Served as Commander of the American army without pay throughout the Revolutionary War against Britain.

🏴 Only he and James Monroe ran for the presidency unopposed.

During His Terms

🏴 Lived in New York but supervised the building of the President's House in the District of Columbia, which later presidents used.

🏴 Bill of Rights became law.

🏴 Departments of State, Treasury, and War started.

FEBRUARY
Brotherhood Week

Brotherhood Week is observed during the week of George Washington's birthday. Its purpose is to further understanding among peoples of all cultures and religions. Brotherhood Week began in 1929 as Brotherhood Day and was the creation of Father McMenamin of Denver, Colorado. By 1946 the day had extended into a week-long celebration.

FEBRUARY 23, 1685
Birth Date of George Frederick Handel

Considered one of the greatest musicians of all times, George Frederick Handel had a rather strange career. He was trained in German music, became a master of Italian opera, and wound up as an Englishman, becoming one of the most important English composers. Handel was a child prodigy born in Halle, Germany. He started learning music at the age of seven. When he was twelve he performed in Berlin at Court, making such an impression that the prince offered to send him to Italy to study music. His father refused to let him go, wanting him to pursue a career in law. Later Handel became a church organist. At twenty, his first opera, *Almira*, was produced in Hamburg. He then went to Italy where he achieved fame as a composer and performer and then on to further success in England. In 1741 he turned from opera to writing oratorios, religious operas usually based on Bible stories. His first, and most successful oratorio, *The Messiah*, is performed at Christmastime and Easter in churches and concert halls throughout the world. Perhaps you can play a recording of the familiar "Hallelujah" chorus from this work today to help the class celebrate Handel's birthday.

FEBRUARY 25, 1913

The Sixteenth Amendment to the United States Constitution, passed by Congress on July 12, 1909, became a law. It provided that Congress had the authority to tax the incomes of citizens. Annually on April 15, Americans file tax returns with the federal government. Older students might examine copies of the federal budget to see how tax dollars are spent.

FEBRUARY 26, 1846
Birth Date of William Frederick Cody—Buffalo Bill

Pony Express rider, Union army scout, Indian fighter, buffalo meat salesman, and international showman are several of the jobs Buffalo Bill worked at during his lifetime. Born in Iowa, Cody was orphaned at eleven and only attended school for a brief period. At an early age he moved to Kansas where he began his multifaceted career as a westerner. In his declining years, after the Indian nations of the West were decimated, Cody organized a

Wild West Show that toured the United States and Europe until 1916, entertaining people who were fascinated with the recently finished era of American history.

Buffalo Bill: Wild West Showman by Mary R. Davidson (Garrard, 1962) is an easy-to-read biography for children.

FEBRUARY 26, 1919

Congress established the Grand Canyon in Arizona as a national park. The park contains 1,052 square miles and is noted for its scenic beauty and wildlife. A group of children might find the names and locations of other national parks. They can put together a bulletin board display using a map of the United States to pinpoint locations and give brief information on each park. Children interested in geology might research the reasons why the Grand Canyon is as deep and colorful as it is.

FEBRUARY 27, 1807
Birth Date of Henry Wadsworth Longfellow

Henry Wadsworth Longfellow's popular poems include "The Song of Hiawatha," "Evangeline," "The Courtship of Miles Standish," "The Village Blacksmith," and the powerful "Paul Revere's Ride." Much of his poetry is written in narrative form and recreates colorful events and figures that shaped American history. A New Englander, the poet taught at Harvard University for almost twenty years. His death in 1882 was mourned throughout America and England. There is a marble bust in the Poet's Corner of London's Westminster Abbey honoring his contributions to world literature.

Paul Galdone has beautifully illustrated Longfellow's *Paul Revere's Ride* (T. Y. Crowell, 1963) in a volume all children will enjoy.

FEBRUARY 29
Leap Year Day

A calendar was introduced by Julius Caesar whose astronomers calculated the year to be 365 days and six hours long. To achieve balance, they added an extra day every fourth year—a slight overestimation! Their error was corrected in 1582. Leap year still occurs every fourth year except in "century years" not divisible by 400. Thus, 1700 and 1900 weren't leap years but 2000 will be. Students can be challenged to find other century years that will not be leap years. An unusual leap year custom to tell the class about is a rather odd old Scottish practice. Since 1288 A.D. the Scotch Parliament has permitted women to collect one hundred pounds in cash from any man refusing their proposal of marriage! France and Italy copied the practice some years afterward.

MARCH

Flower—Daffodil   Birthstone—Bloodstone

Ancient Rome's god of war, Mars, received the honor of opening the Roman new year. March, named after him, was the first month of the Roman calendar until the adoption of the Julian calendar in 46 B.C. The practice of beginning the year with March continued in England and her possessions until the mid-eighteenth century.

POEM OF THE MONTH

THE PASTURE

I'm going out to clean the pasture spring;
I'll only stop to rake the leaves away
(And wait to watch the water clear, I may);
I shan't be gone long.—You come too.

I'm going out to fetch the little calf
That's standing by the mother. It's so young
It totters when she licks it with her tongue.
I shan't be gone long.—You come too.

—Robert Frost

MARCH 1, 1803

Ohio became the seventeenth state to enter the Union.

MARCH 1, 1841
Birth Date of Blanche Kelso Bruce

Blanche Kelso Bruce was born a slave in Prince Edward County, Virginia, but escaped to the North. He attended Oberlin College in Ohio. After the Civil War, he returned to the South and settled in Mississippi. On March 5, 1875, he took the oath of office as United States senator from Mississippi, becoming the second black man to hold this position and the first to serve a full term.

MARCH 1, 1867

Nebraska became the thirty-seventh state.

MARCH 1, 1961

The Peace Corps was established on this date by President John Fitzgerald Kennedy. In 1971 it became part of Action, a new agency that consolidated several volunteer programs. The chief functions of the Peace Corps are to provide skilled manpower to help developing nations and to promote friendship and better understanding between Americans and peoples of other countries. The Corps is manned by volunteers. Any United States citizen over the age of eighteen may apply to serve after passing a physical examination and entrance test. Volunteers are trained while studying the culture and language of the country in which they will serve. The normal tour of duty is two years. Volunteers live in the host countries the same way the native people do.

MARCH 3

Each year on this date the Festival of Dolls, Hina Maisuri, takes place in Japan. This special event is just for girls and lasts for three days. (Boys in Japan have their day too; see May 10 for Boys' Festival.) Girls wear their finest clothes and display collections of treasured ceremonial dolls handed down from generation to generation. The dolls represent the emperor, empress, and their court figures. Five shelves are set up in the best room in the house for the display. The dolls are placed on the shelves in order of importance; the emperor and empress dolls are always placed on the highest shelf. No other dolls are allowed on these shelves; only those packed away for this specific occasion are displayed. Every Japanese girl celebrates her birthday at this time, no matter when it occurs during the year. Girls look forward to entertaining visitors and enjoying these special days.

MARCH 3, 1845

Florida became the twenty-seventh state.

MARCH 3, 1847
Birth Date of Alexander Graham Bell

Alexander Graham Bell was born in Edinburgh, Scotland. His father was a teacher of mutes, and young Bell carried on his father's work in the United States. In 1875, while working with a colleague, Thomas Watson, he accidentally discovered a method of transmitting sound through vibrations. This prompted him to invent an instrument for speaking to people far away—today's familiar telephone! The telegraph, which sent signals via electrified wires, had been invented earlier, but human speech had never been carried by wire until Bell invented the telephone.

He became a United States citizen in 1882 and lived a creative life for many years, giving many services to the deaf and producing other communication devices. A story about him says that he disliked the telephone because it interrupted his experiments!

Children can read about Mr. Bell in *Alexander Graham Bell: Man of Sound,* an easy-to-read biography by Elizabeth Rider Montgomery (Garrard, 1963).

MARCH 3, 1886

Robert Flemming, Jr., a black inventor, was granted a patent for a guitar. In recent years the popularity of this instrument has been revived throughout the world, and it is played by scores of musicians from pop stars to classical performers.

MARCH 4, 1791

Vermont became the fourteenth state.

MARCH 4, 1904
Birth Date of Dr. Seuss

Dr. Seuss' real name is Theodore Seuss Geisel. Since 1937 he has written and illustrated scores of books under two pen names, Dr. Seuss and Theo. Le Sieg (Geisel spelled backwards). He has introduced his readers to such creatures as sneetches, ooblecks, grinches, and gacks. His first book, *And to Think That I Saw it on Mulberry Street* (Vanguard, 1937), was rejected by twenty-nine publishers before it was accepted. Two of his most popular titles, *Cat in the Hat* and *Cat in the Hat Comes Back* (Random House, 1957, 1958) have been read by over three million children and adults. Dr. Seuss currently lives in an observation tower in La Jolla, California.

No matter what grade you teach, find a Seuss book in your school or public library. You won't have to look too hard—just aim for the most dog-eared, well-worn books on the shelves! Or sing, "Happy Birthday Doctor Seuss," while you share his book *Happy Birthday to You!* (Random House, 1959) with the entire class.

MARCH 5, 1770

The Boston Massacre was a pre-American Revolution skirmish between colonial citizens and British soldiers. A crowd had gathered in front of the custom house and were throwing snowballs at the sentries. Friction between Boston's citizens and the British soldiers had been building up for some time, and on the night of March 5, the irritated soldiers fired on the angry mob. Five Americans were killed and six were wounded; one of the dead was Crispus Attucks, a former slave. A monument honoring the five men—the first martyrs of the struggle for American independence—now stands in Boston Commons. In the upper right-hand corner an inscription by John Adams reads, "On that night the foundation of American Independence was laid."

A fine biography for teacher reference is *Crispus Attucks —"The First to Die"* by Edmund F. Curley (Dorrance, 1973). Older girls and boys can learn more about this event in *The Boston Massacre, March 5, 1770: A Colonial Street Fight Erupts into Violence* by Alice Dickinson (Watts, 1968; also in paper).

MARCH 6, 1475
Birth Date of Michelangelo Buonarroti

Michelangelo was one of Italy's—and the world's—greatest artists. Although mainly interested in sculpting large marble statues, he also created paintings, architecture, and poetry. At the age of twelve, after a brief classical education, he became an apprentice to popular fresco painters in Florence and then studied at an art school where he attracted the attention of Lorenzo de'Medici. At age twenty-three he created the famed *Pietà*, the most important work of his youth, which now stands in St. Peter's Church in Rome. His fourteen-foot high sculpture, *David*, was carved from a single block of marble. He was commissioned to paint the ceiling of the Sistine Chapel in the Vatican and completed this magnificent work called *The Creation* in 1510. Twenty-five years later he painted another huge fresco on the end wall of the same chapel, *The Last Judgment*.

The World of Michelangelo—1475–1564 by Robert

Coughlan (Time-Life, 1966) is beautifully and profusely illustrated. Although the text is difficult, students will enjoy looking at the reproductions of his paintings and photographs of his sculptures. Mature readers will enjoy *Michelangelo* by Elizabeth Ripley (Walck, 1953).

MARCH 7, 1849
Birth Date of Luther Burbank

Luther Burbank, an American horticulturist, was a noted breeder of new trees, flowers, fruits, vegetables, grains, and grasses. Among the plants he developed were the Shasta daisy, the spineless cactus, and the white blackberry. He also improved many varieties of plants. Burbank became a gardener to support his widowed mother. His curiosity led him to experiment with plants by crossing (uniting two plants to produce a third) and selecting (choosing the best plants and rejecting inferior ones). He died in 1926 in Santa Rosa, California, where he had lived for more than fifty years and had operated a successful nursery. Parts of Burbank's original acreage in and nearby Santa Rosa can still be visited by the public.

Luther Burbank: Partner of Nature by Doris Faber (Garrard, 1963) can be read by younger readers.

Planting seeds is a good way to celebrate Burbank's birthday. The necessary materials are inexpensive, and children really become excited when sprouts and buds begin to appear, signaling the success of their indoor gardening. You will need small plastic pots, some vermiculite, and the following surefire growers: radish, sunflower, and lima bean seeds that normally germinate rapidly. To speed up the process, soak the seeds for one hour before planting them. Follow-up activities can include graphing growth, keeping records of observed changes, and finding out what various parts of a plant do to insure vigorous growth.

MARCH 9, 1822

The first patent for artificial teeth was granted. It's doubtful that any of your students wears false teeth, but teeth are interesting to study. Use this fact to start a discussion of teeth—real and false. Invite a dentist to the class to talk about teeth and to answer children's questions about false teeth—how they are made, worn, and cared for. The discussion might encourage nonbrushers to take care of their teeth more regularly.

MARCH 10, 1913
Death of Harriet Tubman

Harriet Tubman was born in slavery in Dorchester County, Maryland, about the year 1821. The tablet placed near her home in Auburn, New York, a year after her death beautifully and simply tells the story of her life:

> In memory of Harriet Tubman
> Born a slave in Maryland about 1821.
> Died in Auburn, New York, March 10th, 1913.
> Called the Moses of her people
> During the Civil War. With rare
> Courage she led over three hundred
> Negroes up from slavery to freedom,
> And rendered invaluable service
> As nurse and spy.
> With implicit trust in God
> She braved every danger and
> Overcame every obstacle. Withal
> She possessed extraordinary
> Foresight and judgment so that
> She truthfully said
> "On my Underground Railroad

I nebber run my train off de track
An' I nebber los' a passenger."
This tablet is erected
By the citizens of Auburn.

Children will find the life of Harriet Tubman quite
exciting. The following books will provide information on
her life. For younger readers suggest *Harriet and the Prom-
ised Land* by Jacob Lawrence (Simon and Schuster, 1968).
Older readers will enjoy *Runaway Slave: The Story of
Harriet Tubman* by Ann McGovern (Four Winds Press,
1965; also in paper from Scholastic Book Services and a
book/record combination featuring the book and a 7-inch
LP recording, *Get on Board: Songs of Freedom*). Mature
readers can handle *Harriet Tubman: Guide to Freedom*
by Sam and Beryl Epstein (Garrard, 1968), *Harriet Tubman: Conductor on the Underground Railroad* by Ann
Petry (T. Y. Crowell, 1955), and *Freedom Train: The Story
of Harriet Tubman* by Dorothy Sterling (Doubleday, 1963;
also in paper from Scholastic Book Services).

MARCH 12, 1912

A man parachute jumped from a plane for the first time.
Use this fact to encourage students to list words describing
what it must feel like to parachute from an airplane. The
lists can serve as a basis for children's original stories and
poems.

MARCH 14, 1879
Birth Date of Albert Einstein

Albert Einstein was the physicist who formulated the
theory of relativity that broadened man's understanding of

space, time, and motion. In 1921 he won the Nobel Prize for Physics. He formulated his relativity theory in 1905 when he was only twenty-six years old. Born in Ulm, Germany, Einstein was forced to leave his homeland in 1933 when his German citizenship was taken away by the Nazis because he was Jewish. He developed another revolutionary idea in his new home in the United States. This concept provided the basic principles for making an atomic bomb and other nuclear devices. Einstein's work on the conversion of matter into energy helped bring the world into the atomic age.

MARCH 15, 1767
Birth Date of Andrew Jackson

Seventh President

Born in:	Waxhaw, South Carolina
Occupation:	Lawyer, soldier, planter
President:	1829–1837, Democrat
Died:	June 8, 1845
	The Hermitage, near Nashville, Tennessee

About Jackson

▤ Self-educated on the frontier; nicknamed Old Hickory.

▤ Commanded American forces in victory against English at New Orleans in War of 1812.

▤ Received most popular votes in 1824 presidential election, but John Quincy Adams became president when election was decided by House of Representatives.

During His Terms

▤ President's Mansion renamed White House because of his lack of elegance.

🏳 Westward expansion and focus; Arkansas and Michigan became states.

🏳 Stopped first serious secession move by a state—South Carolina.

🏳 Firm believer in democracy and the rights of the farmer, artisan, and frontiersman.

MARCH 15, 1820

Maine became the twenty-third state.

MARCH 15, 1937

The first blood bank was established in Chicago. Since March is Red Cross Month, you might take this opportunity to have a group of children do research on blood and blood banks and report their findings to the class.

They can learn a great deal about blood in the easy-to-read book *A Drop of Blood* by Paul Showers (T. Y. Crowell, 1967; also in paper and as a filmstrip/record set). If possible, invite a person from the Red Cross to visit the class to discuss the functions of blood banks or have the school nurse visit the class to answer children's questions.

MARCH 16, 1751
Birth Date of James Madison

Fourth President

Born in:	Port Conway, Virginia
Occupation:	Planter, statesman, lawyer
President:	1809–1817, Democratic-Republican
Died:	June 28, 1836
	Montpelier, Virginia

About Madison

- Very frail as a youngster.
- Graduate of Princeton University.
- Member of the Continental Congress and Constitutional Convention.
- Proposed nine of the ten Bill of Rights amendments.
- Served as Jefferson's Secretary of State.

During His Terms

- War of 1812 with England; the British burned President's Mansion in Washington, D. C.
- First protective tariff.
- His wife, Dolley, introduced ice cream as a dessert.

MARCH 17
St. Patrick's Day

According to legend, Saint Patrick was born in the early fourth century A.D. in western England, but no one knows exactly when or where. At age sixteen, he was captured by Irish raiders who carried him to slavery in Ireland. Patrick escaped after six years and entered an English monastery where eventually he became a bishop. He returned to Ireland as a missionary and converted it to Christianity; some historians trace the legend of his driving the snakes out of Ireland to his missionary work. Today celebrations and parades mark the anniversary of his death in 492. It is a national holiday in Ireland and has been celebrated in America since 1737, when a group of Irish Protestants met in Boston to honor St. Patrick and found a group called the Charitable Irish Society.

St. Patrick's Day by Mary Cantwell (T. Y. Crowell, 1967) provides easy-to-read information on this holiday.

MARCH 18, 1806
Birth Date of Norbert Rillieux

Norbert Rillieux, a black scientist, invented a method of refining sugar in 1846 that revolutionized the sugar industry. His techniques were used in Cuba, Mexico, and throughout Europe as well as in the United States. Rillieux was born in New Orleans; he died in Paris, where he lived a good part of his life. In the Louisiana State Museum in New Orleans, there is a memorial to him.

MARCH 18, 1837
Birth Date of Grover Cleveland

Twenty-second and Twenty-fourth President

Born in:	Caldwell, New Jersey
Occupation:	Lawyer, public official
President:	1885–1889, 1893–1897, Democrat
Died:	June 24, 1908
	Princeton, New Jersey

About Cleveland

▧ Sheriff of Erie County, mayor of Buffalo, and then governor of New York State.

▧ Only president to lose a bid for reelection (1888) and run again to win (1892).

During His Terms

▧ Married the youngest first lady in history, twenty-two-year-old Frances Folsom, while in the White House; the wedding march was played by the famous musician John Philip Sousa.

▧ Supported tariff and civil service reform.

▧ Encouraged homesteading by recovering misappropriated lands from the railroads.

[131]

■ During his second term, he faced labor unrest and depression which he alleviated by imposing the gold standard.

■ Developed cancer of the mouth and was forced to wear an upper jaw made of rubber for the remainder of his life.

MARCH 21
First Day of Spring

For some suggestions on welcoming the season, see the entry for September 21.

MARCH 21

The zodiac sign, Aries the Ram, begins today and ends on April 20. How many children in the class were born under this sign?

MARCH 21
No Ruz, Iran's New Year

Houses are cleaned and redecorated, wheat and lentil seeds are planted indoors, small cuttings of shrubbery are set afire in yards for families to jump over, and children go from door to door seeking small gifts. The vernal equinox occurs on March 21, and in Iran spring and the New Year are ushered in together. It is a festive time that lasts for twelve days. During this period people eat special foods such as apples, vinegar, olives, fish, and sweet and sour dishes from a ritual table, the haft-sin, to ensure another year of fertility and well-being for their nation. March 21, 1976, will welcome the year 1355 to Iran.

MARCH 21, 1806
Birth Date of Benito Juárez

Considered the "George Washington of Mexico," Benito Juárez was a Zapotec Indian born in the mountains of Oaxaca. His trials as "Father of His Country" were greater than his North American counterpart, for he not only had to defeat an invading foreign army, but had to contend with political rivals for most of his public life. In 1826 he was elected to Oaxaca's Congress. One of his first acts was to introduce a bill to confiscate the estate of the country's conqueror, Hernán Cortés, with all proceeds to be given over to the state. His opposition to the dictator Santa Anna, conqueror of the Alamo, forced Juárez to flee to New Orleans. When Santa Anna was overthrown, he returned to Mexico and declared himself president.

Juárez's refusal to pay foreign debts gave the French a pretext to invade the country, and he was to flee once again. The French plan was to subjugate the nation sufficiently to proclaim an empire. French troops roamed over northern Mexico searching out Juárez, but he managed to elude them. However, he did send his family to New York City for safety. In May 1864, the Austrian archduke Maximilian arrived with his wife Carlotta to become emperor of Mexico. In 1865 a more significant event happened. In the United States President Johnson made a veiled threat to the French government, complaining that their forces in Mexico violated the Monroe Doctrine. When Juárez's wife visited Washington, she was given a warm reception by Johnson in the White House, his first since taking office. The following year French troops evacuated Mexico City. Juárez and his supporters defeated the diehard Maximilian at Querétaro. Juárez returned to Mexico City in triumph and served as Mexico's president for five years.

MARCH 23, 1775

On this date Patrick Henry delivered his famous "liberty or death" appeal at the Second Virginia Convention. Opposition to British rule of the American colonies was an earmark of this patriot's oratory. Many rich and powerful colonists loyal to the king decried his radicalism, his fight against the Stamp Act, and his treasonous effort to arm the Virginia militia. Henry's words have thrilled generations of Americans:

> Is life so dear, or peace so sweet, as to be purchased at the price of chains and slavery? Forbid it, Almighty God! I know not what course others may take, but as for me, give me liberty, or give me death!

Henry's service to the people continued after independence was won; he became one of the foremost advocates of the Bill of Rights which was amended to the Constitution.

MARCH 24, 1874
Birth Date of Harry Houdini

Harry Houdini, the greatest escape artist who ever lived, was originally named Ehrwich Weiss. The son of a Hungarian rabbi, he was taken from his native Budapest to Appleton, Wisconsin, at an early age. He made his professional debut in a circus in 1883. Inspired by the great French magician, Jean Eugene Robert Houdini (1805–1871), he adopted his name. Houdini's remarkable escapes from handcuffs, straitjackets, prison cells, and submerged boxes earned him world acclaim. He died on Halloween, 1926, in Detroit.

MARCH 25, 1871
Birth Date of Gutzon Borglum

Gutzon Borglum, an American sculptor, is best known for the noted Mount Rushmore Memorial in South Dakota, which features the heads of four United States presidents— George Washington, Thomas Jefferson, Abraham Lincoln, and Theodore Roosevelt. The busts are the largest in the world. Other works by Borglum include the head of Lincoln in the rotunda of the Capitol building in Washington, D. C., and a statue of Lincoln seated on a bench, which is located in Newark, New Jersey. Borglum was born John Gutzon de la Mothe Borglum to Danish parents in Idaho. He died in 1941 before the Mount Rushmore Memorial was completed. His son, who had worked with him, completed the job.

MARCH 26, 1874
Birth Date of Robert Lee Frost

> You know, I've often said that every poem solves something for me in life. I go so far as to say that every poem is a momentary stay against the confusion of the world.*

Poet Robert Lee Frost was born in San Francisco. He did not attend school until he was about twelve years old and never read a book until he was fourteen. His participation in the inauguration of President John F. Kennedy was a highlight in his career. On his eighty-eighth birthday he was awarded the Congressional Medal at the White House

---

* From WGBH Education Foundations and Holt, Rinehart, and Winston, Inc. film, *A Lover's Quarrel with the World*. New York: Holt, 1963.

by President Kennedy. In 1974, a United States ten-cent commemorative stamp was issued to celebrate the one-hundredth anniversary of his birth. Share the poem of the month, "The Pasture," with the class today in honor of the poet's birth. Or dip into the wonderful anthology, *You Come, Too* (Holt, 1959), a selection of Frost's poetry compiled especially for young readers by Nancy Larrick. Middle-graders will enjoy the biography, *Robert Frost: American Poet* by Doris Faber (Prentice-Hall, 1964).

MARCH 27, 1845
Birth Date of Wilhelm C. Roentgen

In 1895, this German physicist discovered X rays—high-frequency short-wave rays produced by a stream of electrons. Medical science has found countless uses for Roentgen's discovery in research, diagnosis, and treatment of disease. Because of his discovery's importance, Roentgen was awarded the Nobel Prize in 1901. Today X rays are measured in units called roentgens, honoring the man who discovered them.

MARCH 29, 1790
Birth Date of John Tyler

Tenth President

Born in:	Charles City County, Virginia
Occupation:	Lawyer
President:	1841–1845, Whig
Died:	January 18, 1862
	Richmond, Virginia

About Tyler

▦ First vice-president to assume full presidential powers after the death of William Henry Harrison.

▦ Champion of states' rights.

During His Term

▰ Whig Party tried to direct him; expelled him when he showed independence.

▰ Weather Bureau started.

▰ Feuded with Congress.

▰ Annexed Texas.

▰ First president to marry while in office; he had been a widower.

MARCH 30, 1870

The Fifteenth Amendment became part of the United States Constitution. It forbids any state to deny citizens the right to vote because of "race, color, or previous condition of servitude."

MARCH 31, 1889

The Eiffel Tower built by Alexandre Gustave Eiffel was completed on this date. Eiffel built the tower for the World's Fair in Paris. At that time it was the tallest building in the world—985 feet high. Today the tower still attracts thousands of visitors and is one of the most famous architectural structures in the world.

MARCH/APRIL
Easter Sunday

For Christians the world over Easter Sunday is the holiest religious holiday of the year. It celebrates the resurrection of Jesus Christ who rose from the dead to new life. Easter Sunday comes on the first Sunday after the first full moon in spring.

The following books will provide both you and your students with additional information on this day. For younger readers suggest *Easter* by Aileen Fisher (T. Y. Crowell, 1968) and *Easter* by Lillie Patterson (Garrard, 1966). For older readers try *Lilies, Rabbits, and Painted Eggs: The Story of Easter Symbols* by Edna Barth (Seabury, 1970) and *It's Time for Easter* by Elizabeth Hough Sechrist and Janette Woolsey (Macrae Smith, 1961).

MARCH/APRIL
Passover

Pesach, the festival of Passover, is an important event in the cultural life of Hebrews and is the best known of the Jewish holidays. It commemorates two events of ancient and historic importance: *1*) Shepherds of old marked the arrival of spring by sacrificing a lamb to insure their flocks' multiplication and *2*) the Hebrews escaped from slavery in Egypt. Jews commemorate these events by holding a family gathering—the Seder—at which the flight of their ancestors is recounted. Special foods are an integral part of the Passover ritual: Matzoh or unleavened bread, a lamb bone, roasted egg, parsley, bitter herbs, salt water, nuts, apples, and wine. The father of the house explains their significance by reading from the Haggadah, a religious account of the Hebrews' Egyptian slave experience in which God forced the Pharaoh to release the enslaved Hebrews. This story is recounted in the Book of Exodus in the Bible.

For further information on this event, children can read *Jewish Holidays* by Betty Morrow and Louis Hartman (Garrard, 1967) and *Passover* by Norma Simon (T. Y. Crowell, 1965).

APRIL

Flower—Sweet Pea   Birthstone—Diamond

Until 45 B.C., April was the second month of the Roman calendar. The meaning and origin of the word *April* is the subject of considerable debate. One authority, Jakob Grimm, stated that it may have originated from the name of a hypothetical god or hero named Aper of Aprus. Others say the name is derived from the verb *apeire* meaning *to open*, referring to the opening of leaves and buds at this time of year.

POEM OF THE MONTH

He capers,
he dances,
he has eyes of youth,
he writes verses,
he smells April and May.

—William Shakespeare from *Merry Wives of Windsor*

APRIL 1
April Fool's Day

"Look! There's a lizard crawling on your desk!"

Not really, but such exclamations are something you may have to put up with today as youngsters walk into the classroom. April Fool's Day originated in France. Prior to the adoption of the Gregorian Calendar in the late sixteenth century, the vernal equinox and the New Year occurred concurrently around April 1. This was a time of festivity and gift exchanging. After the adoption of the new calendar, people far removed from the centers of civilization continued the old practice of celebrating and gift giving. Because of their error, they were ridiculed. In time this changed to April Fool practical joking.

APRIL 1, 1970
Census Day

The Census Bureau used this date to find out how many people live on the 3.5 million square miles of the United States, who they are, and the trends for the future. According to the census report there were nearly 205 million Americans. Other interesting facts to share with students include:

[140]

- A baby is born every 8.5 seconds in the United States.
- A death occurs every 16.5 seconds.
- A new immigrant arrives each 79 seconds.
- Someone leaves the country to take up residence in a foreign land every 23 minutes.
- 74 percent of the population lives in urban areas; 4 out of 5 live in or around cities with populations of 50,000 or more.

The net effect of these changes is an increase in population of about 250 persons every hour. In 1974 the population of the country was over 210 million.

APRIL 2, 1805
Birth Date of Hans Christian Andersen

Hans Christian Andersen was a poet, novelist, and playwright, but he is best known throughout the world for his many delightful fairy tales such as "The Ugly Duckling," "The Emperor's New Clothes," "The Princess and the Pea," and "The Snow Queen," most of which contain a moral. Andersen was the son of a poor Danish shoemaker. At age eleven, after his father died, the boy stopped going to school and spent his time making toys and puppets. At fourteen he journeyed to Copenhagen to become an opera singer. Unsuccessful at this and several other ventures, he turned to writing, and when he was seventeen published his first book, *The Ghost at Palnatoke's Grave*. His first real success came in 1835 with his novel *The Improvisatore*. That same year he also published a first installment of his *Fairy Tales*. More tales appeared the following years, and by 1845 he had written three books of fairy tales, which brought him fame throughout Europe. Although he continued writing novels and plays, they were not as popular as his fairy tales, which are now known and translated all over the world.

In 1872, Andersen had a strange accident. He fell out of bed and injured himself so badly that he never fully recovered. He died three years later.

You'll find many single and collected volumes of Andersen's *Fairy Tales* in your school or public library. Two popular volumes for young readers are *The Ugly Duckling* and *The Ugly Duckling and Two Other Stories* retold by Lilian Moore (Scholastic Book Services, both paper). Children will also enjoy the biography *The Fairy Tale Life of Hans Christian Andersen* by Eva Moore (Scholastic Book Services, paper). Older girls and boys will enjoy *Hans Christian Andersen* by Hedvig Collin (Viking, 1955). Today is a good day to read the class one of Andersen's tales. Their morals can serve as discussion starters in upper grades.

APRIL 5, 1839
Birth Date of Robert Smalls

Robert Smalls was born a slave in Beaufort, South Carolina, a town near the sea. When the Civil War broke out, Smalls was twenty-three years old. His master allowed him to work as a stevedore on the Confederate naval ship, *The Planter*, one of the fastest and most valuable ships in the navy. Smalls devised a daring plan that he shared with the crew. One May day when the crew was alone on the ship, Smalls smuggled his family aboard, lifted anchor, sailed for Charleston Harbor, and turned the vessel over to the Union navy. Smalls received great praise and a large reward for his heroic deed; the following year he was made captain of the ship.

After the war he served in the South Carolina legislature and became a major general in the state militia. From 1875 to 1886 he served three terms in the United States House of Representatives. Southern racists managed to have him jailed for "corruption," but his supporters reelected him to the House. Smalls helped to create the marine base at Parris Island, the training grounds for thousands of Americans who served in the Marine Corps. He died in 1916.

Mature readers in the upper grades can read the exciting biography of Robert Smalls in Dorothy Sterling's *Captain of the Planter* (Doubleday, 1958 also in paper from Pocket Books).

APRIL 5, 1856
Birth Date of Booker Taliaferro Washington

Educator and stateman, Booker T. Washington was Frederick Douglass' successor as the foremost American black leader of his day. Washington was born a slave in Hale's Ford, Virginia. After completing his studies at Wayland Seminary in Washington, D. C., he founded the Tuskegee Institute in 1881 and became its first president. He believed that the road to equality was through education. Tuskegee is now famous throughout the world for agricultural research.

Washington became the first black American to be elected to the Hall of Fame at New York University in New York City. On the base of his bust there are the following lines from one of his speeches:

The highest test of the civilization of a race is
its willingness to extend a helping hand to the
less fortunate.

On April 7, 1940, the Booker T. Washington ten-cent stamp, the first of its kind honoring a black American, went on sale at Tuskegee. The stamp belongs to the Famous American series and bears a picture of the head of Washington. Young philatelists in your class might look for a picture or the stamp itself in their stamp albums. In May 1946, the first coin honoring a black American was issued—a fifty-cent piece bearing a bust relief of Washington. Encourage young numismatists to search for this within their coin collections.

APRIL 6, 1909
Discovery of the North Pole

Robert Peary's expedition reached the North Pole on this date. Persistance carried this naval career officer toward his goal despite several previous failures. Peary's curiosity about the far north was whetted by his 1886 discovery that Greenland was an island. He organized two expeditions to search for the North Pole in 1897 and 1905; both failed! In 1908, his third party, composed of four Eskimos and a fellow American, a black man named Matthew Henson, finally succeeded in reaching the North Pole.

Middle-grade readers who are interested in the Arctic exploration and the men involved will enjoy *Robert E. Peary: North Pole Conquerer* by Erick Berry (Garrard, 1963); two biographies of Matthew Henson include *Ahdoolo! The Biography of Matthew B. Henson* by Floyd Miller (Dutton, 1963) and *To the Top of the World* by Pauline K. Angell (Rand-McNally, 1964).

APRIL 10, 1849

Walter Hunt patented the safety pin. It took him only three hours to develop the idea and to construct a working model for this device that is used for so many different things today. Pass out safety pins to all the children in the class and ask them to list as many uses for them as they can think of.

APRIL 12, 1877

James Tyng, a Harvard catcher, wore the first face protector in baseball. This wire mask, called a "birdcage," was designed by Frederick Thayer, a coach. It was patented and became a forerunner of today's catcher's mask. Students might enjoy listing other athletic protective gear and the reasons athletes wear them.

APRIL 12, 1961

Yuri Gagarin, a Russian cosmonaut, became the first man in space. He made one orbit of the earth aboard the spacecraft *Vostok I.*

APRIL 13, 1743
Birth Date of Thomas Jefferson

Third President

Born in:	Albemarle, Virginia
Occupation:	Farmer, lawyer, public official
President:	1801–1809
Died:	July 4, 1826
	Monticello, Virginia

About Jefferson

- Spoke Latin, Greek, Italian, French, and Spanish.
- One of the authors of the Declaration of Independence.
- Founded Democratic-Republican Party.
- Amateur scientist, architect, inventor, and book collector.
- Left written instructions for design of his gravestone.

During His Terms

- Ended much of the pomp and circumstance surrounding the presidency, including national celebration of presidents' birthdays.
- Authorized the Louisiana Purchase and the explorations of Lewis and Clark.
- Helped plan Washington, D. C., building styles.
- Tripolitan War against pirates in the Mediterranean concluded.
- Protested British seizures of American ships and seamen.

APRIL 13, 1796

America saw its first elephant! It came to New York City from Bengal, India. It was two years old and stood six and a half feet high. You might read the class the very funny poem "Eletelephony" by Laura E. Richards from her book *Tirra Lirra* (Little, Brown, 1932). Young children will delight in the wordless picture book *Elephant Buttons* by Noriko Ueno (Harper, 1973) or the humorous picture book *The Elephant Who Liked to Smash Small Cars* by Jean Merrill and Ronni Solbert (Pantheon, 1967; also in paper).

APRIL 15, 1452
Birth Date of Leonardo da Vinci

When the name Leonardo da Vinci comes to mind, one immediately thinks of his great achievements as a painter and sculptor. These include the portrait of *Mona Lisa*, which hangs in the Louvre Museum in Paris, and *The Last Supper*, a Fresco, in the Santa Maria delle Grazie in Milan. But da Vinci's interests ranged widely. As a scientist he is famous for anticipating important discoveries about blood circulation, the special functions of the brain, and several modern inventions such as the airplane, tank, submarine, and cannon.

Fables of Leonardo da Vinci interpreted and translated by Bruno Nardini (Hubbard Press, 1972) is filled with many short writings by this fifteenth century Italian genius. Mature readers will enjoy the fictionalized biography *Leonardo da Vinci* by Iris Noble (Norton, 1965).

APRIL 18, 1775

Paul Revere began his famous ride to warn the American colonists that "the British are coming." Revere left Boston at about 10:00 P.M. and arrived in Lexington at midnight, riding a borrowed horse, to warn Samuel Adams and John Hancock of the imminent danger. The event inspired Henry Wadsworth Longfellow to write one of his most famous poems, a moving ballad that became one of the best known poems in American literature. The first stanza begins:

> Listen my children, and you shall hear,
> Of the midnight ride of Paul Revere,
> On the eighteenth of April, in seventy-five;
> Hardly a man is now alive
> Who remembers that familiar day and year . . .

[147]

From 1776 to 1779 Revere served as a Revolutionary soldier. He was also a craftsman of note and was the first American to discover the process of rolling sheet copper. He built the first copper rolling mill in the United States. Until that time all sheet copper had been imported. Revere was born in Boston and died there on May 10, 1818.

Younger readers can learn more about the life of this American patriot in *Paul Revere: Rider for Liberty* by Charles P. Graves (Garrard, 1964); older boys and girls can read *America's Paul Revere* by Esther Forbes (Houghton, 1946).

APRIL 18, 1934

The first store equipped with public washing machines in which people could do their laundry opened in Fort Worth, Texas.

APRIL 20, 1898

Pierre Curie (1859–1906) and his wife Marie (1867–1934) uncovered the elements radium and polonium. This team of scientists discovered these elements in pitchblende ore and was awarded the Nobel Prize in Physics in 1903 for their findings. After the death of her husband, Marie Curie took over his professorship at the Sorbonne. Her work on isolating metallic radium won her a second Nobel Prize in 1911, making her the first person to win this award twice. Radium, a radioactive substance, is used to treat cancer; it must be handled with great care. Excessive exposure to radiations causes leukemia (blood cancer).

The Curies' daughter, Irene (1897–1956), inherited her parents' interest in science. She too married a fellow scientist, Frederic Joliot. Together they studied high-energy radiation, and in 1935 they were awarded the Nobel Prize in Chemistry for their synthesis of new radioactive elements. These studies paved the way for the development of nuclear energy.

Ironically, both Marie Curie and her scientist daughter probably died from overexposure to the radioactive substances which they pioneered.

APRIL 21

The zodiac sign, Taurus the Bull, begins today and ends on May 21. How many children in the class were born under this sign?

APRIL 21, 1959

Alfie Dean, a South Australian fisherman, set a record when he hauled in a 2,664-pound, 16-foot, 10-inch, white man-eating shark on a rod with a 130-pound test line. One, or several, of your students may be fishermen or fisherwomen. What are their biggest catches?

APRIL 22, 1774

A group of New Yorkers emulated their compatriots in Boston who dumped a cargo of tea into the harbor on December 16, 1773. Both groups were protesting against the arbitrary tax imposed upon tea by Britain's Parliament. The New Yorkers' act took place without the colorful Indian costumes the Bostonians had used to disguise their action!

APRIL 23, 1564
Birth Date of William Shakespeare

William Shakespeare was probably the greatest English poet and dramatist. His works have such universality that they have been translated into more languages than any book in the world except the Bible. Although Shakespeare wrote for adult audiences, there are many segments within his great body of work that children will enjoy hearing or reading.

Today is a good day to introduce Shakespeare to your class. Even the youngest child can delight in a dramatic reading of his "Song of the Witches" from *Macbeth*.

Round about the cauldron go:
In the poison'd entrails throw.
Toad, that under cold stone
Days and nights has thirty-one
Swelter'd venom sleeping got,
Boil thou first i' the charmed pot.
Double, double toild and trouble;
Fire burn and cauldron bubble.

Fillet of a fenny snake,
In the cauldron boil and bake;
Eye of newt and toe of frog,
Wool of bat and tongue of dog,
Adder's fork and blind-worm's sting,
Lizard's leg and howlet's wing,
For a charm of powerful trouble,
Like a hell-broth boil and bubble.
Double, double toild and trouble;
Fire burn and cauldron bubble.
Cool it with a baboon's blood,
Then the charm is firm and good.

Perhaps the well-known lines from Act II of *As You Like It* can provoke a fresh discussion:

All the world's a stage,
And all the men and women merely players.
They have their exits and entrances;
And one man in his time plays many parts.

Or try the April poem of the month.

Older girls and boys might present a reading of one of his plays. An excellent resource is *Shake Hands with Shakespeare* by Albert Cullum (Citation Press, 1968, paper); it includes eight adaptations for elementary school children of the bard's greatest comedies and tragedies: *Hamlet, Macbeth, Julius Caesar, Romeo and Juliet, The Comedy of Errors, The Taming of the Shrew, A Midsummer Night's Dream,* and *The Tempest*. In addition to the plays, there are scene-by-scene vocabulary lists, hints on how to stress the appropriate mood and theme of each play, and simple costuming and staging suggestions. Student scripts of the individual plays are available or may be purchased in packets of twenty of the same title. If you are looking for a more ambitious project, your class might produce a play by Shakespeare for a school assembly. And if you are extra ambitious, you might plan an annual Shakespeare Festival.

A handsome single volume based on *A Midsummer Night's Dream* is *Bottom's Dream* by John Updike (Knopf, 1969); included within the volume is theme music composed by Felix Mendelssohn. *When Daisies Pied, and Violets Blue: Songs from Shakespeare* by Mary Chalmers (Coward, 1974) presents eight of the bard's most cherished songs enhanced by full-color illustrations. Notes by Shakespearean scholar C. Walter Hodges add to this pleasurable introduction to the beauty of Shakespeare's lyrics. *Seeds of Time: Selections from Shakespeare* compiled by Bernice Grohskopf (Atheneum, 1963) contains brief selections from various plays, poems, and sayings culled from twenty-four of Shakespeare's works. *Tales from Shakespeare* by Charles and Mary Lamb, a classic text first published in 1807, is available in many editions. *Shakespearean Sallies, Sullies, and Slanders: Insults for All Occasions* compiled by Ann McGovern (T. Y. Crowell, 1969) is an entertaining assortment of insults—mainly one-liners—arranged in seventeen parts.

APRIL 23, 1791
Birth Date of James Buchanan

Fifteenth President

Born in:	Cove Gap, Pennsylvania
Occupation:	Lawyer, public official
President:	1857–1861, Democrat
Died:	June 1, 1868
	Lancaster, Pennsylvania

About Buchanan

🏳 Never married but adopted two of his sister's children and a daughter.

🏳 Unsuccessful in three previous presidential bids: 1844, 1848, 1852.

During His Term

🏳 John Brown's raid on Harpers Ferry in Virginia, an anti-slavery protest.

🏳 He advocated buying Cuba for the United States.

🏳 He was unable to handle the slavery problems that were splitting the country.

🏳 Seven Southern states seceded and formed the Confederacy.

APRIL 24, 1704

The first American newspaper, the Boston *News-Letter*, was published by John Campbell, a postmaster. Have the children find the date their local newspaper was founded. How many years after this date did their paper appear?

APRIL 26, 1785
Birth Date of John James Audubon

John James Audubon was born at Le Cayes, Santo Domingo (now Haiti). When still a youngster, his father, a French sea captain, took him to France. After being educated there to become either a soldier or engineer, his father sent him to live in Philadelphia on his estate. Here Audubon found what he described as "a blessed spot, where hunting, fishing, and drawing occupied my every moment."

After marrying, he sold the estate and went into a series of unsuccessful business ventures. At thirty-four he began studying and sketching the different species of American birds. On a trip down the Mississippi River to New Orleans, Audubon drew pictures of native birds. His attempts to publish these in America failed, so he journeyed to England to seek support there. He was able to have his drawings printed in black-and-white and then painstakingly hand-colored the beautiful prints. Eventually a full-color volume, *Birds of America*, was issued. The complete edition contained 435 plates with 1,065 life-sized reproductions of American birds in their characteristic poses and habitats. At a recent auction in London, an original edition sold for $216,000. The volume is acclaimed as the authoritative book on North American birds.

In 1905 the National Audubon Society was established to promote the protection and conservation of birds, wildlife, plants, soil, and water. Its many-faceted educational programs include the Audubon Junior Clubs in schools throughout the United States and Canada and *Audubon Magazine.*

Upper-grade readers can learn more about Audubon in *The Life of Audubon* by Clyde Fisher (Harper, 1949), a biography that includes many reproductions of Audubon's paintings in black-and-white and full color. All readers will enjoy *Let's Discover Birds in our World* by Ada and Frank Graham, Jr. (Western, 1974), one book in a series of Audubon Primers, sponsored by the National Audubon Society. Full-color photographs by Elaine Wickens are included throughout the volume.

APRIL 27, 1822
Birth Date of Ulysses S. Grant

Eighteenth President

Born in:	Point Pleasant, Ohio
Occupation:	Soldier
President:	1869–1877, Republican
Died:	July 23, 1885
	Mount McGregor, New York
	Buried in New York, New York.

About Grant

◼ By the time he was eighteen, his name had changed three times. He was originally Hiram Ulysses Grant, which he later changed to Ulysses Hiram Grant, but ended up with Ulysses S. Grant because of an error on his West Point appointment.

◼ Rose from Civil War captain to the commander of the Union army who accepted Lee's surrender on April 3, 1865, at Appomattox Courthouse in Virginia.

During His Terms

🚩 Charges of mismanagement made against him because he appointed friends to high posts; widespread corruption prevailed.

🚩 First transcontinental railroad completed in 1869.

🚩 Homestead Act permitted western lands to be settled by land-hungry pioneers.

APRIL 28, 1758
Birth Date of James Monroe

Fifth President

Born in:	Westmoreland County, Virginia
Occupation:	Lawyer
President:	1817–1825, Democratic-Republican
Died:	July 4, 1831
	New York, New York
	Buried in Richmond, Virginia

About Monroe

🚩 While serving as Washington's Minister to France, he freed Thomas Paine from prison there.

🚩 Only president other than Washington to run unopposed.

During His Terms

🚩 Flag of the United States was adopted.

🚩 Florida sold to the United States by Spain in 1819.

🚩 Monroe Doctrine promulgated, keeping Europeans out of the Western Hemisphere.

APRIL 28, 1788

Maryland became the seventh state to ratify the Constitution.

APRIL 29
Japanese Emperor's Birthday

World War II marked the end of the Japanese emperor's sanctified, absolute rule. Today in Nippon, or the Land of the Rising Sun as Japanese people call their nation, the emperor's position is symbolic and ceremonial. The imperial family is highly regarded, continuing a two thousand year tradition, and on the emperor's birthday a great celebration takes place. Religious ceremonies, colorful parades, and a march past the Imperial Palace in Tokyo mark the event as the Japanese people pay tribute to their emperor's special position.

Marking this occasion can give youngsters insight into the broad variety of political systems people have devised for governing themselves. Upper-grade students, as individuals or groups, can research and report on some contemporary political systems such as dictatorship, democracy, fascism, communism, constitutional monarchies, and the United States balance of powers.

APRIL 30, 1803

Napoleon, the ruler of France, concluded the largest real estate transaction in world history—the Louisiana Purchase. Facing the threat of imminent war with Great Britain, Napoleon sold the French territory of Louisiana to agents of President Thomas Jefferson for about four cents an acre, a total of fifteen million dollars. The vast area, 827,987 square miles, stretched from the Gulf of Mexico to Canada, and from the Mississippi River to the Rocky Mountains. Jefferson, who had only intended to purchase the key port city of New Orleans, engaged two army officers to conduct the first exploration of the American Northwest. These two men, Captain Meriwether Lewis and Lieutenant

William Clark spent the years from 1804 to 1806 mapping the area. They encountered unknown Indian tribes, new types of flora and fauna, and led their small expedition across an area of great natural beauty.

A group of upper-grade students can present a program on Lewis and Clark's epic journey, tracing their route to the Pacific. Several might clarify their concept of area by actually measuring a square mile area in their immediate community. Their experience will highlight the significance of Jefferson's "bargain." A complete account of the explorers' adventures appears in a book geared to middle-grade readers, *The Lewis and Clark Expedition, 1804–1806: The Journey That Opened the American Northwest* by Dan Lacy (Watts, 1974).

APRIL 30, 1812

Louisiana became the eighteenth state.

APRIL/MAY
Arbor Day

In today's ecology-conscious world Arbor Day takes on more meaning than ever before. In the mid-1800s, B. G. Northrup, chairman of the American Forestry Association, suggested that schools set aside a day each year for planting trees. His idea worked! Today Arbor Day is observed in every state. Check your calendar for the date in your state. Though there is no specific date because climates and conditions vary too greatly, it is usually celebrated in late April or early May.

If possible, contact a local greenhouse or nursery and ask it to donate a small tree to be planted on or near the school grounds. A tree planting ceremony can involve all

[157]

the classes in the school. A committee of children can plant the tree with the aid of the school custodian. Give the tree a name to honor someone and invite classes to walk by the newly planted tree at various times during the day. Such a ceremony might lead to a discussion of trees—what uses they have, varieties, and so on.

The younger children will enjoy hearing or reading *A Tree Is Nice* by Janice May Udry (Harper, 1956). This book won the 1957 Caldecott Award for Marc Simont, the illustrator. A useful and practical book for young readers is *Trees and How We Use Them* by Tillie S. Pine and Joseph Levine (McGraw-Hill, 1969). Besides presenting a wealth of information about trees, the authors provide simple, lively experiments the children can try.

A different type of book is *Once There Was a Tree: The Story of the Tree, A Changing Home for Plants and Animals* by Phyllis S. Busch (World, 1968; also in paper from Scholastic Book Services). This easy-to-read text, illustrated with many fine black-and-white photographs by Arline Strong, tells the fascinating story of how a tree changes during its life cycle and the many different kinds of living things that live in it, on it, under it, and around it. Part of World's "Discovering Nature Series," this volume will motivate children to explore and discover the world of nature on their own.

Your Friend, the Tree by Florence M. White (Knopf, 1969) discusses fifteen specific types of trees and their uses, for example, ponderosa pine, the tree used for building homes and furniture, sugar maple, the tree "that makes your pancakes good," and banana, the tree that is not a tree! Older readers will learn a great deal from this inform- ative, yet easy-to-read text. *Arbor Day* by Aileen Fisher (T. Y. Crowell, 1965) relates the origins of the holiday.

MAY

Flower—Lily of the Valley   Birthstone—Emerald

May's name and the number of days it contains have a mixed history. The name can be traced back to Maia, the goddess of "growth and increase." Some authorities, however, maintain that May was named to pay tribute to the Majores or Maiores, the older branch of the Roman Senate. The number of days has varied from twenty-two to thirty to today's thirty-one. Romans associated this month with flowers, fertility, and the rich gifts of nature.

❖❰

POEM OF THE MONTH

How pleasant to know Mr. Lear!
  Who has written such volumes of stuff!
Some think him ill-tempered and queer.
  But a few think him pleasant enough.
His mind is concrete and fastidious,
  His nose is remarkably big;
His visage is more or less hideous,
  His beard it resembles a wig.
He has ears, and two eyes, and ten fingers,
  Leastways if you reckon two thumbs;
Long ago he was one of the singers,
  But now he is one of the dumbs!

—Edward Lear

MAY 1
May Day

May Day originated in the rites of the ancient Romans and Druids who called upon nature during this period to bring forth another life-giving spring. Trees were a central object of worship in their rituals. The English changed the custom by erecting maypoles in villages around which all danced and frolicked. They transformed the day into such a spirited festival that Puritan leaders barred the celebration in the mid-seventeenth century. Today May Day is celebrated in most areas of the world as a spring festival. In the Soviet Union and other communist nations it is a day to honor labor and arouse support for the communist and socialist causes. This practice was started in the United States in the nineteenth century by an early radical trade union, the Knights of Labor.

May Day by Dorothy Les Tina (T. Y. Crowell, 1967) is an easy-to-read book describing the origins of this holiday.

MAY 1, 1931

The Empire State Building was opened to the public. The skyscraper, located on Fifth Avenue in New York City, is one of the tallest buildings in the world. It has 102 stories and towers 1,250 feet high; a 222 foot television tower brings the total height to 1,472 feet—more than a quarter of a mile high. Each year over one and one-half million people visit the building's two large observatories on the eighty-sixth and one hundred second floors. The Empire State Building was the tallest building in the world until the World Trade Center opened in New York City in 1972. Both these buildings are now surpassed in height by the Sears Tower in Chicago, which opened in 1974.

Let's Go to Build a Skyscraper by Augusta Goldin (Putnam, 1974) explores in simple terms and illustrations the construction and function of skyscrapers of the future.

MAY 3, 1898
Birth Date of Golda Meir

When she was eight, Golda Meir's family moved from Kiev, Russia, to Milwaukee, Wisconsin. She attended the Teachers' Seminary there and later became a leader in the Milwaukee Labor Zionist party. While still young she and her husband immigrated to Palestine and lived on a kibbutz. She became active in politics and labor and served in many governmental capacities, including that of Israel's first ambassador to Moscow. In 1969 Ms. Meir became prime minister of Israel, a position she held until her formal resignation on June 5, 1974.

MAY 6, 1931
Birth Date of Willie Mays

Willie Mays has become one of the most exciting base-ball players in history. In 1969 he became the second player in major league history to hit more than 600 home runs. In 1970 Mays made his 3,000th hit, making him the tenth player to accomplish this feat. He has also led the National League four times in stolen bases. Mays retired from his baseball career in September 1973, after bringing more than two decades of joy to baseball fans.

Middle-grade readers will enjoy *The Baseball Life of Willie Mays* by Lee Greene (Scholastic Book Services, paper).

MAY 7, 1840
Birth Date of Peter Ilich Tchaikovsky

Tchaikovsky was one of Russia's first composers to gain international fame. He began composing seriously when he was twenty-six and produced symphonies, concertos, operas, and overtures. His ballet scores have become classics. These include *Swan Lake, Sleeping Beauty*, and *Nutcracker*. His famous overtures include *1812* and *Romeo and Juliet*. In 1891 he visited the United States and was received with great enthusiasm. He died two years later in St. Petersburg, which is now Leningrad.

Older girls and boys who are interested in music will enjoy *The Pantheon Story of Music for Young People* by Joseph Wechsberg (Pantheon, 1968). Celebrate Tchaikov-sky's birthday with the class by playing a selection or two from *Nutcracker*. Perhaps several of your students have seen a production of the ballet, which is popular around Christmastime.

MAY 8, 1884
Birth Date of Harry S. Truman

Thirty-third President
      Born in: Lamar, Missouri
      Occupation: Businessman, public official
      President: 1945–1953, Democrat
      Died: December 26, 1972

About Truman
  ▥ Small-town background where he was "Mr. Average Citizen."
  ▥ Hardships of Depression years ended his small haberdashery business leading him to politics and the Senate.
  ▥ As vice-president during Roosevelt's fourth term, he succeeded to the office upon the president's death.

During His Terms
  ▥ Made decision to use atomic bomb against Japan on August 6, 1945, at Hiroshima and three days later at Nagasaki.
  ▥ Inaugurated Truman Doctrine in post-World War II period against communist expansion in Europe.
  ▥ Won reelection in 1948 against Republican Thomas E. Dewey, New York's governor, despite all polls showing he would lose.

MAY 9, 1800
Birth Date of John Brown

John Brown's passionate anti-slavery stance was inherited from his father, Owen, an active abolitionist who sheltered runaway slaves. John Brown and his five sons moved to the Kansas Territory in 1855 and took part in the widespread fighting between pro- and anti-slavery forces in that area. On October 16, 1859, together with twenty-one other zealots, Brown made his most daring move—the capture of a United States government arsenal at Harpers Ferry, Virginia. With the arms they seized, the band hoped to spark slave revolts all over the South. Colonel Robert E. Lee, who later served as a general for the Confederacy, led the U.S. Marines who captured Brown and his men. Brown was hanged in December, but he was considered by many to have been a martyr. Less than eighteen months after his death Union soldiers marched off to fight in the Civil War singing a song praising John Brown. Sing the song, "John Brown's Body" which today goes:

> John Brown's body lies a-moldering in the grave,
> John Brown's body lies a-moldering in the grave,
> John Brown's body lies a-moldering in the grave,
> His soul is marching on.
>
> Glory, glory, hallelujah!
> Glory, glory, hallelujah!
> Glory, glory, hallelujah!
> His soul is marching on!

John Brown's Raid by Lorenz Graham (Scholastic Book Services, 1972; also in paper) gives a pictorial history of the attack on Harpers Ferry; the text is profusely illustrated with maps, photographs, and drawings.

MAY 9, 1914
Mother's Day

Mother's Day became a public holiday. Julia Ward Howe, who wrote the words to "The Battle Hymn of the Republic" (see May 27), is said to have been the first to suggest a Mother's Day in the United States in 1872. For many years previously the English had been honoring mothers on a day called Mothering Sunday; other countries had also been observing similar days. In 1915 President Woodrow Wilson signed a joint resolution of Congress recommending that Mother's Day be a holiday. He proclaimed it an annual observance to be held on the second Sunday in May.

Younger readers can learn how this holiday came to be in *Mother's Day* by Mary Kay Phelan (T. Y. Crowell, 1965).

MAY 10

Boys' Festival is a holiday celebrated in Japan and Hawaii. Large carps made of paper or cloth are flown from tall poles. Families having one or more boys fly a carp for each one—the largest carp represents the oldest, the smallest, the youngest. Carp signifies strength and courage because it swims upstream and against strong currents. Boys also display treasured dolls on this festival day—dolls that represent ancient warriors and heroes. Girls, too, have their day in Japan (see March 3 for the Festival of Dolls).

MAY 11, 1858

Minnesota became the thirty-second state.

MAY 12, 1812
Birth Date of Edward Lear

Edward Lear, the man whose name is synonymous with limericks, was born in London, the youngest of twenty-one children. Early in life he became an artist, painting birds and illustrating the works of naturalists. At twenty-one he published a large collection of colored bird drawings. While doing similar work for the Earl of Derby, he lived at the earl's home where he became popular with the children of the family because of the absurd poems and drawings he created for them. These became the nucleus of his *Book of Nonsense* (1846). Later Lear moved to Italy, where he continued to write and illustrate books, mainly about his travels.

All children enjoy the whimsy of Mr. Lear. The youngest will love his nonsense alphabet, which begins:

A was once an apple-pie,
> Pidy
> Widy
> Tidy
> Pidy
> Nice insidy
> Apple-Pie.

A paperback edition of the complete alphabet, *A Was Once an Apple-Pie*, illustrated by William Hogarth, is available from Scholastic Book Services. Five- and six-year-olds will delight in the hilarious *The Owl and the Pussycat*. A sparkling edition of this narrative poem is illustrated by William Pene du Bois (Doubleday, 1962). Older children will enjoy *The Quangle Wangle's Hat*, illustrated by Helen Oxenbury (Watts, 1969) and *The Scroobious Pip*, illustrated by Nancy Ekholm Burkert (Harper, 1968). The handwritten manuscript of this poem was discovered in a nearly finished state among Lear's papers after his death. This edition has been completed by Ogden Nash. All of Lear's humorous writing is contained in *The Complete Nonsense Book*, edited by Lady Strachey (Dodd, Mead, 1942).

Share some Lear limericks with the class. Here is one:

There was a Young-Lady whose chin
Resembled the point of a pin;

So she had it made sharp,
And purchased a harp,
And played several tunes with her chin.

Also enjoy the May poem of the month, a ditty Lear wrote about himself. Students might try to create limericks of their own. The form consists of five lines. Lines one, two, and five rhyme; lines three and four may or may not rhyme. Mature readers can find out more about this talented "human bean" in *Mr. Nonsense: A Life of Edward Lear* by Emery Kelen (Nelson, 1973).

MAY 12, 1820
Birth Date of Florence Nightingale

Florence Nightingale, the founder of modern nursing, was named for Florence, Italy, where she was born while her wealthy British parents were living there. Nightingale was one of the greatest women of England's Victorian Age. During the Crimean War (1854), British soldiers referred to her as "The Lady with the Lamp" because of her constant devotion—night and day—to aiding the wounded. Within five months after her arrival in the Balkans, the military death rate fell from 40 to about 2 percent. Her work was even celebrated in a poem written by Henry Wadsworth Longfellow. When the war ended in 1856, she returned to England. Though quite ill, she continued to work to improve the nursing profession through writing and lecturing. Shortly before her death in 1910, King Edward VII presented her with the Order of Merit; she was the first woman to be so honored.

Younger readers can read the story of her life and work in *Florence Nightingale: War Nurse* by Anne Colver (Garrard, 1961).

MAY 14, 1908

Charles W. Furnas became the first passenger to fly in an airplane. He flew with Wilbur Wright on a flight that lasted 28.6 seconds. (See also August 19.)

MAY 14, 1948

Israel became an independent nation. Have a child in the class locate Israel on a world map and compare its size with one of the United States. Many children will be amazed to find out that Israel is just about the size of New Jersey. Which of the United States are bigger? Which are smaller?

MAY 15, 1930

Ellen Church, a registered nurse, became the world's first airline stewardess on a Boeing 80A trimotor flight from San Francisco to Cheyenne, Wyoming. She and seven other registered nurses were hired by United Airlines. Today airlines call stewardesses flight attendants. Perhaps you can invite a local flight attendant to come to the class to answer children's questions about flight travel and the duties plane crews perform in the skies.

MAY 19, 1925
Birth Date of Malcolm X

Malcolm X, born Malcolm Little, became famous as a leader of the black religious movement named the Nation of Islam (Black Muslims). Many Muslims took the letter X as a last name to reject the family names given by white owners to their slaves. Malcolm X rose from a sordid and squalid background to become a powerful spokesman for black nationalism. In 1964 he formed the Organization of Afro-American Unity—a protest movement that advocated separation of the races to unify, dignify, and reshape the character of the black masses. The following year, at age thirty-nine, Malcolm X was shot and killed while delivering a speech to his followers in New York City. His dedication to his people is admired by many Americans.

Children can read more about his life and work in the easy-to-read biography *Malcolm X* by Arnold Adoff (T. Y. Crowell, 1970; also in paper).

MAY 20–21, 1927

Charles Lindbergh made the first solo flight across the Atlantic Ocean in his plane, *The Spirit of St. Louis.* He flew from Roosevelt Field on Long Island, New York, to Le Bourget Field near Paris. The flight of about 3,610 miles was made in $33\frac{1}{2}$ hours. His definitive account of the flight, *The Spirit of St. Louis* (1954), won the 1954 Pulitzer Prize in American biography.

Born in Detroit, Charles Augustus Lindbergh had always been interested in air travel. In 1920 he entered the University of Wisconsin as a mechanical engineering student but left in 1922 to enroll in a flying school in Lincoln, Nebraska. In 1924 he entered the United States Air Service Reserve and graduated with the rank of second lieutenant the following year. He made his first professional flight as an air mail pilot.

Older children can read more about Lindbergh in *Ride on the Wind* by Alice Dalgleish (Scribner, 1956).

MAY 22

The zodiac sign, Gemini the Twins, begins today and ends on June 21. How many children in the class were born under this sign?

MAY 23, 1788

South Carolina became the eighth state to ratify the Constitution.

May 23, 1975

Junko Tabei, a Japanese housewife, became the first woman to reach the top of Mt. Everest, the highest mountain in the world. A member of an expedition of fifteen Japanese women, she reached the summit of the 29,028-foot mountain by taking the southeast route used by Sir Edmund Hillary and Sherpa Tenzing Norgay, the first to scale Everest in 1953. Thirty-three men have climbed Mt. Everest since then.

MAY 24, 1626

Peter Minuit bought Manhattan Island, which later became part of New York City, from the Indians for the equivalent of $24—a good buy at anytime!

MAY 25, 1895
Birth Date of George Herman (Babe) Ruth

714 is the magic number associated with this baseball hero who was named the greatest player in the game's history by the Baseball Writer's Association of America in 1967. After a childhood of poverty in Baltimore, one of his teachers recognized his baseball skill and helped him

start his career in 1914. Babe first won acclaim as a pitcher for the Boston Red Sox. In the 1920s he joined the New York Yankees where he won the love of the fans by breaking fifty world records. He batted in 2,209 runs and only one man has succeeded in equaling his 714 home run total— Henry Aaron.

Middle-graders can learn how Babe Ruth and four other great players made baseball history in *Baseball: Hall of Fame, Stories of Champions* (Scholastic Book Services, paper). Mature readers will enjoy *The Babe Ruth Story* (Scholastic Book Services, paper) as told to Bob Considine. An interesting comparison of Babe Ruth and Henry Aaron's baseball careers appears in *The Home Run Kings* by Clare and Frank Gault (Scholastic Book Services, 1974).

MAY 27, 1819
Birth Date of Julia Ward Howe

Born in New York City, Julia Ward Howe was a writer, lecturer, and social reformer. Moved by the plight of Civil War widows, she worked for women's rights in the professions and business. She authored books on many different subjects including drama, verse, biography, and travel. Howe introduced the idea of Mother's Day in America (see May 9) and wrote the words to "The Battle Hymn of the Republic" to the tune of "John Brown's Body" in 1861. It was published in the Atlantic Monthly and soon became the war song of the Union forces. She married Dr. Samuel Gridley Howe, another American social reformer.

MAY 29, 1790

Rhode Island became the thirteenth state to ratify the Constitution.

MAY 29, 1848

Wisconsin became the thirtieth state.

MAY 29, 1917
Birth Date of John Fitzgerald Kennedy

Thirty-fifth President

Born in: Brookline, Massachusetts
Occupation: Congressman, senator
President: 1961–1963, Democrat
Died: November 22, 1963
Dallas, Texas
Buried in Arlington, Virginia

About Kennedy

▨ Son of wealthy, political family.

▨ PT boat commander in World War II.

▨ Won 1957 Pulitzer Prize for *Profiles in Courage*.

▨ First Roman Catholic president. Won election by narrow margin of 118,550 votes.

During His Term

▨ Started "New Frontier" program of social legislation.

▨ Encouraged Southern black voter registration.

▨ "Bay of Pigs" invasion of Cuba and Soviet missile crisis.

▨ Assassinated in Dallas on November 22, 1963.

MAY 30
Memorial Day

This day was first observed on May 30, 1868, when it was initiated to honor Civil War veterans. Memorial Day, by presidential proclamation, is now observed on the last

[172]

Monday in May when the graves of all American soldiers are decorated with flowers.

MAY 30, 1903
Birth Date of Countee Cullen

The poet, Countee Cullen, was born Countee Porter in Baltimore. Orphaned at an early age, he was adopted by Reverend Frederick Cullen in New York City. After attending public school, Cullen went on to New York University and then to Harvard University, where he received a Master of Arts degree. *Color*, his first volume of poetry, was published in 1925 while he was still a student. His *The Lost Zoo* (Harper, 1940) is considered a children's classic. All children will enjoy these funny poems. A new edition was published by Follett in 1968 with illustrations by Joseph Low. At the time of his death in January 1946, Cullen was a teacher of French at a public high school in Harlem. Five years later the 136th Street Branch of the New York Public Library was renamed for him.

MAY 31, 1819
Birth Date of Walt Whitman

The United States themselves are essentially the greatest poem.
—Walt Whitman

Walt Whitman, an American poet, wrote *Leaves of Grass*, a collection considered one of the world's major literary works. It sings the praises of the United States and of democracy. Whitman began working on *Leaves of Grass* in 1848. Since no publisher would issue it, he brought out his own edition containing only twelve poems in 1855.

[173]

Between this time and his death in 1892, he published several revised editions. One of his frequently quoted poems, "There Was a Child Went Forth," begins:

> There was a child went forth every day,
> And the first object he look'd upon,
>   that object he became,
> And that object became part of him for the day
>   or a certain part of the day,
> Or for many years or stretching cycles of years.

Some of his *Leaves of Grass* poems can be used with upper-grade children. A handsome edition published in paperback by Viking Press contains a lengthy introduction to the poet's life and work written by Malcolm Cowley. All children will delight in *Overhead the Sun: Lines from Walt Whitman* illustrated in full-color woodcuts by Antonio Frasconi (Farrar, Straus, 1969) and *I Hear America Singing* illustrated by Fernando Krahn (Delacorte, 1974).

✦《

JUNE

✦《

Flower—Rose   Birthstone—Pearl

Like April, June's name is also a matter of some debate.
Some authorities believe the name honors Juniores, the
lower branch of the Roman Senate; others claim it is con-
nected with the Consulate of Junius Brutus or with Juno,
wife of Jupiter, king of the gods. Originally June had
twenty-six days. Rome's first king, Romulus, added four
more to it; Numa Pompilius took one from it; Julius
Caesar restored the total to thirty days.

✦《

POEM OF THE MONTH

RUDOLPH IS TIRED OF THE CITY

These buildings are too close to me.
I'd like to PUSH away.
I'd like to live in the country,
And spread my arms all day.

I'd like to spread my breath out, too—
As farmers' sons and daughters do.

I'd tend the cows and chickens.
I'd do the other chores.
Then, all the hours left I'd go
A-SPREADING out-of-doors.

—Gwendolyn Brooks

JUNE 1, 1070

It is recorded that on this date cheese makers in southern France learned to make what is now known as Roquefort cheese. Nearly all cheeses, except cheddar, cottage, and cream cheese, are referred to as foreign-type cheeses in the United States because their production methods originated in other countries. Roquefort is one of them, of course; it is called blue cheese when made in America. Today more than 485 million pounds of foreign-type cheese is made in the United States; approximately ninety million pounds are imported.

This might be a good day for a cheese-and-cracker party in the classroom.

JUNE 1, 1792

Kentucky became the fifteenth state.

JUNE 1, 1796

Tennessee became the sixteenth state.

JUNE 3, 1904
Birth Date of Charles Richard Drew

Charles Drew was an important black surgeon who is chiefly known for his research on blood preservation and for the development of blood banks. He served as a professor and head of the Howard University surgery department and as chief surgeon at Freedman's Hospital in Washington, D. C., from 1941 until his death in 1950.

Middle-graders can read more about him in *Charles Drew* by Jo Polsena (T. Y. Crowell, 1970) and in *Charles Richard Drew: Pioneer in Blood Research* by Richard Hardwick (Scribner, 1967).

JUNE 5, c. 469 B.C.
Birth Date of Socrates

Socrates, the wisest of the Greek philosophers, left no writings of his own. Fortunately his pupil, Plato, recorded his eloquent dialogs with intellectual men of the time. Socrates was born and lived in Athens. His teachings reflected his ethical views; he was entirely devoted to seeking truth, beauty, and goodness. Yet he had many enemies, and in 399 B.C. he was sentenced to death by the rulers of ancient Athens for supposedly corrupting the youth of the city with his ideas. He accepted his fate and peacefully drank a cup of hemlock poison.

Several quotes from Socrates' teachings can be shared to start class discussions:

> Know thyself.
> Courage is knowing what not to fear.

[177]

The nearest way to glory is to strive to be what
you wish to be thought to be.

Nothing can harm a good man, either in life or
after death.

JUNE 7, 1917
Birth Date of Gwendolyn Brooks

The poet deals in words with which everyone is
familiar. We all handle words. And I think the
poet, if he wants to speak to anyone, is con-
strained to do something with those words so
that they will "mean something," will *be* something that a reader may touch.*

Gwendolyn Brooks was born in Topeka, Kansas, but at
an early age moved to Chicago where she still resides. Ms.
Brooks is best known for her poetry for adults. In 1950
she became the first black to win the Pulitzer Prize for
Poetry for her book *Annie Allen* (Harper, 1949). Recently
she was named Poet Laureate of the State of Illinois, suc-
ceeding the late Carl Sandburg. She has only written one
volume of poetry for children, *Bronzeville Boys and Girls*
(Harper, 1956); the June poem of the month, "Rudolph Is
Tired of the City," is from this collection. Each poem in
the book expresses a poignant feeling for children living in
American inner cities.

Teachers and mature readers in upper grades can read
her autobiography, *Report from Part One* (Broadside Press,
1972).

---

* Gwendolyn Brooks. *Report from Part One.* Detroit, Mich.: Broadside
Press, 1972, p. 148.

JUNE 8, 1786

On this date ice cream was first advertised and sold in America. Ice cream has been eaten since 64 A.D. when Nero Claudius Caesar was emperor of Rome, but it wasn't until the end of the eighteenth century that several retail establishments in New York City began to sell it. Dolley Madison is credited with being the first woman to serve ice cream in the White House; it was a favorite dessert at Mount Vernon, the home of George and Martha Washington.

In 1848 Nancy Johnson invented a freezer that changed the future of ice cream. In 1851 Jacob Fussell established the first wholesale ice cream factory in the world. At the corner of Hillen and Exeter Streets in Baltimore, a plaque erected by the Maryland Historical Society reads in part: "Birthplace of the Ice Cream Industry." Share some of these other facts about ice cream with the children—perhaps while eating some on this June day:

· The ice cream cone was introduced in 1904 at the World's Fair in St. Louis, Missouri.

· More than 7 percent of all milk products in the United States is used by the ice cream industry.

· More than 15,000 manufacturers produce more than 100 million gallons of ice cream each year.

· The United States consumes more ice cream than any other country.

Children will enjoy reading additional facts about the history of ice cream and other popular goodies in Solveig Paulson Russell's delightful and informative book *Peanuts, Popcorn, Ice Cream, Candy and Soda Pop and How They Began* (Abingdon, 1970).

JUNE 8, 1869
Birth Date of Frank Lloyd Wright

Many outstanding buildings throughout the world bear the stamp of Frank Lloyd Wright, an innovator in the field of architecture. Born in a small Wisconsin town, Wright brought his love of nature to architecture. His aim was to meld a structure and its surroundings into a unified entity, and his buildings achieved this goal. He also introduced new materials, such as pre-cast concrete, and new concepts of space and use of mass produced items. His works ranged from residential homes to office buildings to churches to factories to an ultramodern plan for a mile-high skyscraper. Among the buildings he designed were a house jutting out over a waterfall at Bear Run, Pennsylvania, the Imperial Hotel in Tokyo, Japan, and the Guggenheim Museum in New York City.

JUNE 11, 1880
Birth Date of Jeannette Rankin

Born and brought up on a ranch near Missoula, Montana, Jeannette Rankin was the first woman to be elected to the House of Representatives. She served two terms—1917–1919 and 1941–1943—as a Republican Congresswoman from Montana. Active throughout her life in the women's suffrage and pacifist movements, she was the only member of Congress to vote against both World War I and World War II.

JUNE 12, 1963

Medgar Wiley Evers, a black civil rights leader, was assassinated in Jackson, Mississippi. Evers was field secretary of the National Association for the Advancement of Colored People (NAACP) in Mississippi. He worked to help blacks politically by encouraging them to register to vote.

JUNE 14, 1777
Flag Day

According to legend Betsy Ross created the first United States flag when she sewed together the stars and stripes in 1776. On June 14, 1777, her design was accepted, and a resolution was adopted by the Continental Congress, ". . . that a flag of the United States be thirteen stripes, alternate red and white, that the 'Union' be thirteen stars, within a blue field, representing a new constellation." The resolution did not, however, specify the arrangement of the thirteen stars on the blue field. After the admission of Kentucky and Vermont, another resolution was adopted in January 1794, making the flag one of fifteen stars and fifteen stripes.

Realizing the flag would become unwieldly with a stripe for each new state, Captain Samuel C. Reid of the United States Navy suggested to Congress that the number of stripes remain the same (thirteen) to represent the original colonies and that a star be added to the blue field for each new state joining the Union. A law to this effect was passed on April 4, 1818. The flag of the United States had changed many times since this date. The last change was made on July 4, 1960, when the fiftieth star representing Hawaii was added.

Flag Day by Dorothy Les Tina (T. Y. Crowell, 1965) provides an easy-to-read account of the holiday.

JUNE 15, 1215

On this date the Magna Carta was granted. The Magna Carta or Great Charter is a document that marked a decisive step in the development of constitutional government in England. In it King John of England was compelled to grant many rights to the English aristocracy. The Magna Carta confirmed feudal traditions and defined the limits of an English king's powers, thus preventing the development of absolute monarchy in England.

Four original copies of the charter are still in existence; two are in the British Museum in London.

JUNE 15, 1752

On this date Benjamin Franklin reached out into the heavens to prove that lightning was a form of electricity. Scientists of Franklin's time called the electrical discharges that pass from one storm cloud to another, or between a cloud and the earth, "electrical fire." People believed these fiery flashes had magical qualities. Franklin and his son, William, thought the discharges were a form of natural electricity. They built a special, silk handkerchief kite with which they proved their point at considerable risk. The kite had a piece of wire attached to its tip, which served as a lightning rod that conducted the storm's electrical energy down the string to a key attached several feet above the holder's hand. Standing in an open field, the two guided the kite into a dark storm cloud above. As the storm's intensity developed, the elder Franklin rapped the key with his knuckles. Suddenly sparks leapt from the key. Electrical energy had been drawn from the sky above! Franklin's findings brought him great acclaim; he was invited to discuss his discovery at gatherings of world scientists. (See also January 17, 1706.)

Independent research by students will reveal many items of interest concerning Benjamin Franklin. One group might present a many-faceted portrait of the man's achievements as an author, statesman, and signer of both the Declaration of Independence and the United States Constitution.

JUNE 15, 1836

Arkansas became the twenty-fifth state.

JUNE 16, 1963

Valentina Tereshkova became the first and as yet the only space woman when she began her three-day, forty-eight orbit flight in *Vostok VI*. The twenty-six-year-old Russian cosmonaut had been a textile worker whose hobby was parachuting. She wrote to the directors of the Soviet space program volunteering to train for space flight, and they accepted. Older readers will enjoy reading *It is I, Sea Gull: Valentina Tereshkova, First Woman in Space* by Mitchell R. Sharpe (T. Y. Crowell, 1975). Do any girls in your class want to become female astronauts?

JUNE 17, 1775

The Battle of Bunker Hill began. After the first shots of the War for Independence were fired at Lexington and Concord, Continental troops laid siege to Boston. When British reinforcements arrived, American troops stationed themselves upon Breed's Hill overlooking Boston. Although outnumbered, they withstood two assaults by General Howe's men on their outpost. Then their ammunition gave out, and they were forced to retreat when the British seized the hill in their third attack. This conflict became known as the Battle of Bunker Hill. In 1825 a monument was dedicated at the site in the presence of the Marquis de Lafayette who was visiting the United States, a nation he had helped create (see September 9, 1757).

JUNE 17, 1972
Watergate Day

The arrest of five burglars in the offices of the Democratic National Committee in the Watergate building complex in Washington, D. C., just five months prior to the presidential election, began a scandal that rocked the American political structure and led to President Richard M. Nixon's resignation in August 1974. Nixon's landslide victory over Senator George McGovern in the 1972 election failed to prevent the facts from emerging. The president's closest advisors had organized a group called "the plumbers" who regularly indulged in wiretapping and other illegal acts. Officials of the Nixon administration and the president himself attempted to deny these activities. It took over two years of Senate hearings, several special prosecutors, grand jury trials, impeachment proceedings, the revelation of White House tape recordings, and a ruling by the Supreme Court that these tapes must be surrendered to reveal the truth to bring about the downfall of the Nixon presidency. Many leading Nixon associates were sentenced to jail terms for their roles in what were called "the White House horrors" and subsequent attempts to cover them up.

JUNE 19, 1846

"One—two—three strikes you're out!" These words might have been yelled at the first recorded baseball game played in Hoboken, New Jersey. This date is considered the beginning of organized baseball in the United States.

JUNE 19, 1910
Father's Day

Father's Day was first celebrated in Spokane, Washington. In 1924 President Calvin Coolidge recommended that the day be observed as a holiday in all states. Traditionally Father's Day is held on the third Sunday in June, and it is a day for all to do something special for their fathers.

JUNE 20, 1863

West Virginia became the thirty-fifth state.

JUNE 21,
First Day of Summer

For some suggestions on welcoming the season in, see the entry for September 21.

JUNE 21, 1788

New Hampshire was the ninth state to ratify the Constitution.

JUNE 22

The zodiac sign, Cancer the Crab, begins today and ends on July 23. How many children in the group were born under this sign?

JUNE 24, 1916
Birth Date of John Ciardi

John Ciardi is one of America's foremost contemporary poets. His translation of Dante's *Divine Comedy* brought him international recognition. Since 1955 he has been poetry editor of *Saturday Review*. Mr. Ciardi's poetry appeals to primary children as well as adults. Young children will enjoy *I Met a Man* (Houghton, 1961), the poet's own favorite book, which was written on a first-grade vocabulary level for his daughter, Myra, and *The Reason for the Pelican* (Lippincott, 1959). Older girls and boys will delight in his modern fable, *John J. Plenty and Fiddler Dan* (Lippincott, 1963), the story of a grasshopper and an industrious ant. Mr. Ciardi can be heard reading his works on several recordings available from Spoken Arts, Inc.: *You Read to Me, I'll Read to You* and *You Know Who/John J. Plenty and Fiddler Dan and Other Poems*.

JUNE 25, 1788

Virginia was the tenth state to ratify the Constitution.

JUNE 27, 1872
Birth Date of Paul Laurence Dunbar

Paul Laurence Dunbar was an American novelist and poet. His father escaped from slavery in Kentucky prior to the Civil War and settled in Dayton, Ohio, where young Dunbar was born and died thirty-two years later. He was one of the first writers to portray black life with realism. All his poetry is contained in *The Complete Poems of Paul Laurence Dunbar* (Dodd, Mead, 1965). This edition also includes the famous William Dean Howells' preface on Dunbar, which did so much to bring him to the attention of readers everywhere. In 1975 a United States commemorative stamp was issued honoring this famous black American writer.

JUNE 27, 1880
Birth Date of Helen Keller

Despite several handicaps, Helen Keller became an author, lecturer, and educator. She suffered a severe illness before she was two years old that left her blind and deaf. When she was seven, she was placed in the care of Annie Sullivan of the Perkin's Institute for the Blind, and by the time she was ten, she had learned to speak. Ten years later, with Ms. Sullivan, she attended Radcliffe College where she graduated with honors. Throughout her life she traveled and lectured extensively. After Ms. Sullivan's death in 1936, Ms. Keller's new companion was Polly Thomson; she had become her secretary in 1914. Ms. Keller authored many books, bringing her message of courage and hope to the handicapped everywhere. Several of her titles include *The Story of My Life* (1903), *The World I Live In* (1908), and *Let Us Have Faith* (1940). She died in Westport, Connecticut, at the age of eighty-eight.

Middle-graders can read further about this incredible American woman in *Helen Keller* (Scholastic Book Services, paper) and *Helen Keller's Teacher* (Four Winds, 1965; also in paper from Scholastic Book Services) both written by Margaret Davidson. More mature readers can handle Helen Keller's own *The Story of My Life* (Scholastic Book Services, paper), the autobiography she wrote when she was a junior in college.

JUNE 29, 1577
Birth Date of Peter Paul Rubens

Born in Seigen, Germany, Peter Paul Rubens became one of the greatest Flemish painters of the 1600s. Besides creating paintings, tapestries, occasional illustrations for books, architecture, and sculpture, he was also a noted scholar and respected diplomat. The ancient Roman sculpture he studied in Italy in 1600 as well as the works of the Renaissance artists Michelangelo and Raphael influenced his style. His paintings are known for their monumental scale, brilliant colors, and feeling of movement and vitality. During his lifetime he completed an enormous amount of work dealing with a variety of subjects such as hunting scenes, landscapes, biblical and mythical episodes, and portraits.

JUNE 30, 1859

Imagine walking across Niagara Falls—that roaring chasm between New York State and Canada. People have! They have sailed over the falls, which drop 500,000 tons of water a minute, in flimsy barrels; they have used rafts and barges, but a French tightrope walker, Blondin, is remembered as the greatest daredevil of all. On this date he made his first crossing on a rope 1,100 feet long. In July he repeated the amazing feat several times adding new obstacles—Blondin carried a man on his back, he pushed a wheelbarrow, and for a finale he sat down in the middle of his rope and cooked an omelette. The great high ropewalker started performing on ropes as an infant of six and continued until he was seventy-two.

JULY

Flower—Larkspur   Birthstone—Ruby

Originally the seventh month was the fifth on the Roman calendar. It was called Quintilis meaning *fifth* and had thirty-six days. Romulus reduced the number to thirty-one, Numa Pompilius cut it back to thirty, and later Julius Caesar restored one day giving it thirty-one. Marc Anthony complimented Julius Caesar by naming the month July after him as Caesar's birthday fell on the fourteenth. The month became officially July in 44 B.C., the year Caesar was stabbed and killed by Brutus.

POEM OF THE MONTH

LANDSCAPE

What will you find at the edge of the world?
A footprint,
a feather,
desert sand swirled?
A tree of ice,
a rain of stars,
or a junkyard of cars?

What will there be at the rim of the earth?
A mollusc,
a mammal,
a new creature's birth?
Eternal sunrise,
immortal sleep,
or cars piled up in a rusty heap?

—Eve Merriam

JULY 1, 1863

The Battle of Gettysburg began. General Robert E. Lee was ready to make his second attempt to invade the North, and he marched with his troops to the town of Gettysburg, Pennsylvania. When a group of soldiers rode ahead of him in search of supplies, they ran into the Union cavalry. The battle that started by chance lasted for three days. It was one of the bloodiest of the entire Civil War, but it was the turning point that led eventually to victory for the Union army. (See November 19 for Lincoln's Gettysburg Address.)

JULY 2, 1908
Birth Date of Thurgood Marshall

Thurgood Marshall studied dentistry at Lincoln University but then changed his mind and entered Harvard University Law School where he graduated at the top of his class in 1933. On October 2, 1967, President Lyndon Baines Johnson appointed him the first black justice of the United States Supreme Court.

JULY 3, 1890

Idaho became the forty-third state.

JULY 4, 1776
Independence Day

The United States celebrates its birthday on this day, which commemorates the signing of the Declaration of Independence by members of the Second Continental Congress meeting in Philadelphia. The American Fourth of July is one of the oldest independence days in the world. The Declaration of Independence, written by Thomas Jefferson, was eventually signed by fifty-five other men in defiance of Britain's King George III who threatened them with death for their action.

Two of the foremost early American leaders, John Adams and Thomas Jefferson, both past presidents, died on July 4, 1826, the fiftieth anniversary of the nation they helped to conceive.

Many special events have taken place in the United States on this date:

1817—Ground was broken for the Erie Canal.
1828—The Baltimore and Ohio Railroad began operating.

1832—"America" was sung for the first time.
1848—The Cornerstone of the Washington
Monument in Washington, D. C. was laid.
—The first Women's Rights Convention
met at Seneca Falls, New York.
1858—The first baseball series began.
1861—The Battle of Bull Run was fought.
1863—Vicksburg surrendered.
—Battle of Gettysburg was fought.
1884—The United States received an important
birthday gift—The Statue of Liberty.

The Fourth of July by Mary Kay Phelan (T. Y. Crowell,
1966) and *Fourth of July* by Charles P. Graves (Garrard,
1963) give additional information on this great patriotic
holiday.

JULY 4, 1872
Birth Date of Calvin Coolidge

Thirtieth President
    Born in: Plymouth, Vermont
    Occupation: Farmer, lawyer
    President: 1923–1929, Republican
    Died: January 5, 1933
              Northampton, Massachusetts
              Buried in Plymouth, Vermont

About Coolidge
    ■ Became president upon Harding's death while in
office.
    ■ Father administered oath of office in a Vermont
farmhouse.

During His Terms

🏳 Called "Silent Cal" because of his conservative retiring manner.

🏳 Encouraged business expansion and government's noninterference in stock market.

JULY 7, 1881
Birth Date of Pinocchio

Carlo Lorenzini, whose pen name was Collodi, published his classic tale *Pinocchio*, which is about a puppet who comes to life. There are many versions of this story available. One of the loveliest modern editions is the large-sized *The Adventures of Pinocchio* (Macmillan, 1969). It is illustrated by Attillio Mussino whose artwork has been hailed as the perfect interpretation of the story and earned him a gold medal at the International Exposition at Turin, Italy, in 1908.

JULY 8, 1835

The Liberty Bell cracked while tolling the death of Chief Justice John Marshall. The Liberty Bell has become a symbol of the American fight for independence because it was rung on July 8, 1776, to announce independence. The large metal bell, which weighes 2,080 pounds, was brought to Philadelphia in 1752 from England. It bears the inscription from the Bible's Book of Leviticus: "Proclaim Liberty throughout all the land unto all Inhabitants Thereof."

During the British occupation of the city (1777–1778) the bell was moved to Allentown, Pennsylvania, and hidden under the floor of a church for safety. After its return to Philadelphia, it was rung on Independence Day and on other special occasions—until it cracked! On D Day, June 6, 1944, during World War II, the bell was tapped by the mayor, and the tone was broadcast by radio throughout the nation.

JULY 10, 1875
Birth Date of Mary McLeod Bethune

Mary McLeod Bethune, a black educator, founded the Bethune-Cookman College in Daytona, Florida, a school that grew into one of the largest institutions for training black teachers in the southeastern United States. During the Depression of the 1930s, Ms. Bethune worked with President Roosevelt to help young people. She served as the director of the Negro Affairs Division of the National Youth Administration, an organization that helped more than half a million black students stay in school during these difficult years. Ms. Bethune died on May 18, 1955. Part of her last will and testament reads:

> I leave you love; I leave you hope; I leave you the challenge of developing confidence in one another; I leave you a thirst for education; I leave you a respect for the use of power; I leave you faith; I leave you racial dignity; I leave you a desire to live harmoniously with your fellow men; I leave you a responsibility to our young people.

JULY 10, 1890

Wyoming became the forty-fourth state.

JULY 11, 1767
Birth Date of John Quincy Adams

Sixth President

Born in: Braintree, Massachusetts
Occupation: Lawyer, statesman
President: 1825–1829, Democratic-Republican
Died: February 23, 1848
Washington, D.C.
Buried in Braintree, Massachusetts

About Adams

▨ Foreign service as United States minister to the Netherlands, Sweden, Britain, Germany, Portugal, and Russia.

▨ Elected president by the House of Representatives— of four candidates running in 1824, none won a majority of the Electoral College vote.

▨ Leading anti-slavery advocate.

▨ After his presidential term, he served as a congressman for seventeen years in the House of Representatives.

During His Term

▨ Great rivalry with Andrew Jackson, who received the largest popular vote in the presidential election. Adams was the only president in history who did not have the congressional support of a political party, and he could accomplish little.

JULY 14, 1789
Bastille Day

Today is Bastille Day in France. On this date citizens of Paris stormed the royal prison, the Bastille, where political enemies of the king were imprisoned. The prison had become the hated symbol of the king's absolute power. The French were emulating the struggle of American colonists who had achieved independence from Britain in 1776, and the taking of the Bastille signaled the beginning of the French Revolution. Today in France, Bastille Day is celebrated with mammoth parades, the display of the tricolor flag, and the singing of "La Marseillaise," the national anthem.

JULY 14, 1913
Birth Date of Gerald R. Ford

Thirty-eighth President

      Born in: Omaha, Nebraska
      Occupation: Lawyer
      President: 1974–   , Republican

About Ford

▀ Son of divorced parents.

▀ Name changed from Leslie King, Jr. to Gerald Rudolph Ford, Jr. when his mother remarried.

▀ Football player; linebacker and center on the University of Michigan team; offered professional contract in 1932–1933.

▀ Conservative Republican congressman.

▀ Member of the Warren Commission that investigated assassination of President Kennedy.

▀ Chosen as vice-president-designate by Nixon after resignation of Agnew. First appointed vice-president in history, October 1973.

▀ Became president when Nixon resigned on August 10, 1974 because of his Watergate involvement and certain impeachment.

▀ First United States president not elected by the people.

JULY 15

An English saying goes:

> St. Swithin's Day, if thou dost rain,
> for forty days it will remain;
>
> St. Swithin's Day, if thou be fair,
> for forty days 'twill rain nae mair.

St. Swithin was buried, so legend tells, by his own request in the churchyard of Winchester Cathedral in England. When he was made a saint, the monks decided to move his body into the Cathedral. This event took place on July 15, a day when it rained heavily. The rain kept falling for the next forty days, leading many people to believe that St. Swithin would have preferred to be out in the open. Look out for rain today!

JULY 16, 1945

The first atom bomb was exploded at Alamogordo Air Force Base in a desolate portion of New Mexico. After Germany's surrender in early May 1945, the Allies still faced a long, arduous war against Japan. To shorten the conflict they issued an ultimatum telling the Japanese "the alternative to surrender is prompt and utter destruction." When this peace initiative was rejected, President Harry S. Truman authorized the use of the new weapon. On August 6, 1945, an atomic bomb was dropped on Hiroshima; more than 160,000 people were killed or injured. Three days later the city of Nagasaki was similarly destroyed. The Japanese surrendered on August 14. World War II was ended by the most devastating weapon mankind has ever developed.

Mature readers in the upper grades will learn a great

deal about this event and its aftermath from *Return to Hiroshima* by Betty Jean Lifton (Atheneum, 1970). The text is illustrated with photographs by Eikoh Hosoe, a Japanese photographer.

JULY 19, 1916
Birth Date of Eve Merriam

> When something is too beautiful or too terrible
> or even too funny for words, then it is time for
> poetry.*

Eve Merriam lives in New York City with her author-husband, Leonard C. Lewin, two sons, and a family cat named Towel. Ms. Merriam always wanted to be a poet, and while in school her work was published in a variety of student publications. Her first book of adult poetry, *Family Circle* (Yale University Press, 1946), won the Yale Younger Poets Prize. Other books followed in rapid succession, including nonfiction children's books and poetry for adults and children.

Ms. Merriam can be heard reading several of her poems for children on the recording *To Catch a Little Rhyme* (Caedmon, distributed by D. C. Health), a record that invites children to respond both verbally and with their whole bodies. Her trilogy *Catch a Little Rhyme* (1966), *It Doesn't Always Have to Rhyme* (1964), and *There Is No Rhyme for Silver* (1962; all Atheneum) will be enjoyed by all children. Particularly suitable for upper-grade children are *Out Loud* (1973) and *Independent Voices* (1968, both Atheneum), a book of seven longer poems about people in history such as Benjamin Franklin, Ida B. Wells, Frederick Douglass, and Lucretia Mott. The July poem of the month,

---

* From *Inside a Poem*, a brochure published by Atheneum.

"Landscape," appears in *Finding a Poem* (Atheneum, 1970). Older children will enjoy reading her essay in this volume, "Writing a Poem," which describes how she creates a poem from start to finish.

JULY 20, 1969

A man monitoring a receiver in Houston, Texas, heard one of mankind's most historic messages: "Tranquility Base here. The Eagle has landed." *Apollo 11*'s lunar module, Eagle, had set down upon the moon's Sea of Tranquility. Six hours later the first human set foot upon the lunar crust and declared, "That's one small step for a man, one giant leap for mankind." Neil A. Armstrong relayed these words to earth shortly before he was joined by his copilot, Colonel Edwin E. Aldrin, Jr., of the Air Force. Together Armstrong and Aldrin explored a small area around the module. A worldwide audience witnessed these first steps across the powdery surface as the spacemen planted an American flag and gathered rock samples. Man had attained an ancient dream—space exploration had become a reality.

JULY 24, 1898
Birth Date of Amelia Earhart

Amelia Earhart, a famous American aviator, was the first woman to cross the Atlantic in an airplane (1928), to fly over the Atlantic alone (1932), to make a nonstop flight across the United States (1932), to fly from Hawaii to California (1935), and to receive the Distinguished Flying Cross. During her lifetime she also established both altitude and transcontinental speed records. On July 1, 1937, she set out from Miami for a flight around the world. On July 3, her airplane disappeared in the South Pacific Ocean. No positive trace has ever been found of her or her plane. Ms. Earhart was declared dead in 1939.

JULY 24

The zodiac sign, Leo the Lion, begins today and ends on August 23. How many children in the group were born under this sign?

JULY 25, 1952

Puerto Rico became a commonwealth. Puerto Rico's history and culture are a synthesis of the varied peoples and events that have affected this island in the West Indies. Arawak Indians, Spaniards, and Americans have all ruled it. Self-government was withheld by the United States, which acquired the island after the Spanish-American War, until the 1950s. Puerto Ricans then wrote their own constitution and chose to be associated with the United States as a commonwealth rather than as a state. Today statehood or independence are serious questions Puerto Ricans are discussing.

The First Book of Puerto Rico by Antonio J. Colorado (Watts, 1972) provides a fine introductory history for upper-grade students. After they have learned about the island, they might want to debate the question whether or not Puerto Rico should become the fifty-first state.

JULY 26, 1788

New York became the eleventh state to ratify the Constitution.

JULY 26, 1965

Britain granted independence to the Maldive Islands. Older children can locate these islands, which lie four hundred miles southwest of Ceylon in the Indian Ocean. After they have found them, they might research the Maldivian word *atoll*. Atolls are coral clusters built entirely of the skeletons of sea animals; when these organisms die, their naturally cemented remains form the foundation of many coral isles.

JULY 28, 1973

Skylab II was launched from Cape Kennedy, Florida. Its crew spent a record-breaking fifty-nine days in space. Navy Captain Alan L. Bean shared the adventure with two others, Major Jack Lousma of the Marines and a civilian scientist, Dr. Owen Garriott. Their flight covered twenty-four million miles and surpassed *Skylab I*'s twenty-eight-day journey around the earth. On September 25, 1973, the spaceship splashed down. Have a group of students do research on man's exploration of space.

JULY 31, 1790

The first federal patent issued by the United States was granted to Samuel Hopkins of Vermont for a process for making potash and pearl ash for soapmaking. Today more than 100,000 inventors contact the United States Patent Office each year. To obtain a patent, inventions must be both new and useful. Approximately 70,000 patents ranging from the ridiculous to the sublime are issued annually. Among them are a self-cleaning blackboard, a pair of shoes with sundial tops by which the wearer can tell the time of day, and a hula hoop with an orbiting satellite. Other inventions that have received patents include Patent 2,947,013 for an audible toothbrush that makes musical sounds when teeth are brushed in a vertical direction and Patent 3,600,728 for a bed that makes itself.

Children might look toward the future and "invent" their own products. They might provide a written description of their idea and accompany it with a diagram or drawing showing how it works. Anyone for a talking cereal bowl that says "Good morning?"

AUGUST

Flower—Poppy   Birthstone—Sardonyx

Julius Caesar's adopted nephew and heir, Gaius Julius
Caesar Octavianus, was the first Roman emperor to receive
the title Augustus, meaning *reverend*, from the Senate.
The senators changed the name of the sixth month of their
calendar, Sextilis, to August to honor their leader. Augustus took a day from February to give his month thirty-one
days so that it would be as long as July, which honored
Julius Caesar.

POEM OF THE MONTH

AUGUST

Mike says
we ought to have
a swimming party.

Fine, I answer,
but where will we
have this party?

Here, he say,
pointing to the fire hydrant.
Here, he says,
when we turn it on.

We'll have a party
and invite
Alex and
any guy who wants to swim

Stand-
ing
up.

—Myra Cohn Livingston

AUGUST 1, 1876

Colorado became the thirty-eighth state.

AUGUST 2, 1873

The inventor Andrew Hallidie piloted San Francisco's
first cable car down Nob Hill at 5:00 A.M. He chose this

early morning hour for a very good reason—there would be fewer people around if anything went wrong. Fortunately, nothing did!

AUGUST 7, 1904
Birth Date of Ralph Johnson Bunche

Ralph Bunche was born in Detroit, the grandson of a slave. Today Dr. Bunche is an internationally famous diplomat and United Nations mediator. In 1950 he became the first black American to receive the Nobel Peace Prize for his many years of working for peace throughout the world and particularly for his role in settling the Arab-Israeli dispute of 1950.

Younger readers can learn more about his many contributions to both America and the world in *The Picture Life of Ralph J. Bunche* by Margaret B. Young (Watts, 1968). Mature upper-graders will enjoy *Ralph Bunche: A Most Reluctant Hero* by James Haskins (Hawthorn, 1974).

AUGUST 10, 1821

Missouri became the twenty-fourth state.

AUGUST 10, 1874
Birth Date of Herbert C. Hoover

Thirty-first President

Born in: West Branch, Iowa
Occupation: Engineer
President: 1929–1933, Republican
Died: October 20, 1964
New York, New York

About Hoover

▰ From poverty to mining engineer in Australia and China, he became a millionaire mine owner.

▰ Humanitarian relief work during and after World War I.

During His Term

▰ Stock Market crash in October 1929 marked beginning of the Great Depression.

▰ By 1932, twelve million Americans were unemployed. He refused to sanction relief measures and relied on individual initiatives to overcome the financial crisis.

AUGUST 17, 1786
Birth Date of David (Davy) Crockett

In 1836, when the ruins of the Alamo were searched, the diary of a legendary frontiersman, David Crockett, was found. It related how 187 Texans had fought to the death against the superior forces of Mexican dictator Antonio López de Santa Anna. Crockett, an Indian scout, army officer, and congressman from Tennessee for three terms, died as he had lived, immersed in adventure. After growing up in Tennessee, Crockett plunged into frontier life where he hunted bears, fought Indians, and cast aside the fetters of town life.

AUGUST 17, 1926
Birth Date of Myra Cohn Livingston

Myra Cohn Livingston was born in Omaha, Nebraska. When she was eleven, her family moved to California, where she still lives in Beverly Hills with her husband and three children. In addition to her writing life, Ms.

Livingston teaches classes in creative writing and lectures extensively on writing and poetry throughout the country. For an exciting discussion of creative writing and the ways the author has used it with children, see her adult book, *When You Are Alone/It Keeps You Capone* (Atheneum, 1973).

For younger readers Ms. Livingston has written many volumes of poetry including *Wide Awake* (1959) and *The Moon and the Star* (1965; both Harcourt), compiled the anthology, *Listen Children Listen: An Anthology of Poems for the Very Young* (Atheneum, 1972), and has written the picture book, *Come Away* (Atheneum, 1974) with beautiful illustrations by Irene Haas. Older students will enjoy *The Way Things Are and Other Poems* (Atheneum, 1974) and *Mailbu and Other Poems* (Atheneum, 1972); the poem of the month, "August," is from this text. Her anthologies include *A Tune Beyond Us* (Harcourt, 1968), *Speak Roughly to Your Little Boy: A Collection of Parodies and Burlesques, Together with Original Poems* (Harcourt, 1971), and *What a Wonderful Bird the Frog Are: An Assortment of Humorous Poetry and Verse* (Harcourt, 1973).

AUGUST 18, 1934
Birth Date of Roberto Clemente

Born in the little town of Carolina, Puerto Rico, Clemente pursued a baseball career from his early childhood. He was spotted on the island in 1954 by the National League's Brooklyn Dodgers and was assigned to their Montreal farm team. After joining the Pittsburgh Pirates, he helped that team become world champions in the World Series of 1960 against the New York Yankees, and again in 1971, playing against the Baltimore Orioles. Clemente was a four-time batting champion of the National League and one of eleven men in baseball history to make 3,000 hits. The star's death in a plane crash on December 3, 1972, brought grief to baseball fans. Clemente had been helping victims of the massive earthquake in Managua, Nicaragua; the plane he was on was carrying relief supplies to the stricken city where 10,000 people lay dead and 200,000 were homeless. Clemente's later election to the Baseball Hall of Fame testified to this player's greatness.

An easy-to-read, illustrated biography of this baseball giant is *Roberto Clemente* by Kenneth Rudeen (T. Y. Crowell, 1974).

AUGUST 19
National Aviation Day

To mark the birth date of Orville Wright, today is celebrated as National Aviation Day. When one thinks of aviation, the Wright brothers, Orville and Wilbur, immediately come to mind. They were mechanics and pilots who pioneered in aviation. They made their first flight in a power-driven aircraft near Kitty Hawk, North Carolina, on December 17, 1903. The plane, driven by a small gasoline engine, had a wingspan of forty feet, six inches. Orville piloted the first of four flights. He was in the air for twelve seconds and covered 120 feet. Wilbur followed with a thirteen-second flight of 195 feet. Then Orville flew more than 200 feet in fifteen seconds. The fourth, and final flight, with Wilbur at the controls, was the most successful—852 feet in fifty-nine seconds. The aircraft can be seen in the National Air Museum in Washington, D. C. Here is the telegraph message Orville sent to his father:

> Success four flights Thursday morning all
> against twenty-one-mile wind started from level

with engine power alone average speed through
air thirty-one miles longest fifty-nine seconds
inform press home Christmas

The Wright Brothers: Kings of the Air by Mervyn D.
Kaufman (Garrard, 1964) relates further details of the
lives and accomplishments of these two inventive men.
Older boys and girls will enjoy *The Wright Brothers at
Kitty Hawk* by Donald J. Sobol (Scholastic Book Services,
paper); it describes three difficult years of trial and error
before their successful flight. Children interested in airplane travel today will enjoy *Ready for Take-off: How
an Airplane Flies and How It Is Flown* by Robin Lawrie
(Pantheon, 1973). This is a book reluctant readers might
enjoy because of the simple format and stylized cartoon
drawings.

AUGUST 20, 1833
Birth Date of Benjamin Harrison

Twenty-third President

Born in:	North Bend, Ohio
Occupation:	Lawyer
President:	1889–1893, Republican
Died:	March 13, 1901
	Indianapolis, Indiana

About Harrison

▰ His grandfather was William Henry Harrison, ninth
president of the United States.

▰ He lost the presidential election by 100,000 popular
votes but won in the Electoral College against Grover
Cleveland.

During His Term

▰ A weak leader with no program of his own.

■ United States population expanded westward; North and South Dakota, Montana, Washington, Idaho, and Wyoming became states.

■ First Pan-American Conference.

■ White House wired for electricity.

AUGUST 21, 1936
Birth Date of Wilt Chamberlain

Wilton Norman Chamberlain was born in West Philadelphia. By the time he entered high school, he was already 6 feet 11 inches tall, two inches short of his present height. He is considered the most famous basketball player in the world. His athletic skills earn him about $200,000 per year, the same salary the president of the United States receives. He was the first athlete in the entire history of sports to earn that much money.

A fine, easy-to-read biography of this basketball giant is *Wilt Chamberlain* by Kenneth Rudeen (T. Y. Crowell, 1970).

AUGUST 24

The zodiac sign, Virgo the Virgin, begins today and ends on September 23. How many children in the group were born under this sign?

AUGUST 25, 1927
Birth Date of Althea Gibson

This world famous tennis star developed many of her skills on a city street in New York's Harlem. Ms. Gibson was twice the women's singles lawn tennis champion of the

United States. In 1957–1958 she reached the peak of her career by winning three championships—the women's singles and doubles at Wimbledon, England, and the United States women's singles.

Tennis is a popular sport. How many of the children you work with are tennis enthusiasts? Several might tell about the game and demonstrate some basic tennis skills to the rest of the group. If it isn't too hot today, it might be a good time to ask, "Tennis, anyone?"

AUGUST 26, 1920

The Nineteenth Amendment giving women the right to vote went into effect.

AUGUST 26, 1974
Women's Equality Day

Women's liberation has become a topic everyone talks about today. Children can be encouraged to discuss their feelings about what women's liberation means to them. Why not introduce the subject by describing the background of this day marking the passage of the Nineteenth Amendment granting women the right to vote. President Ford invited all sixteen female members of Congress to witness his signing the bill that designated the celebration of this day.

A group of children can be asked to report on progress toward adoption of the Equal Rights Amendment, which must be ratified by thirty-eight states by 1979 if it is to become part of the Constitution. It outlaws discrimination based on sex.

AUGUST 27, 551 B.C.
Birth Date of Confucius

Confucius was an ancient Chinese philosopher who devoted many years to thinking and studying about man, his place in the universe, and his relationship to other men. As a young man he organized a school where others could study academic subjects as well as examine duty, love, manners, and how they relate to human life. Some of Confucius' thoughts are embodied in his oft-quoted "sayings." Confucius' real name was K'ung Ch'iu. Confucius is a Latin form of the title K'ung-fu-tzu, which means Great Master K'ung. Although Confucius received some minor official appointments during his lifetime, at the time of his death, he was largely unknown throughout China. His disciples spread his teachings. None of his writings were preserved, but his conversations and sayings were compiled by his followers in a book titled *The Analects*.

AUGUST 27, 1908
Birth Date of Lyndon Baines Johnson

Thirty-sixth President

Born in:	Stonewall, Texas
Occupation:	Congressman, senator, rancher
President:	1963–1969, Democrat
Died:	January 22, 1973

About Johnson
- Texas ranch background.
- Elementary school teacher.
- First congressman to enter the armed forces in World War II.
- Leader of the Senate.
- Became president when John Fitzgerald Kennedy was assassinated.

During His Terms

▦ The 1964 Civil Rights Bill outlawed racial discrimination in public accommodations and employment.

▦ Won the 1964 election against Senator Barry Goldwater by the largest number of votes up to that time.

▦ "Great Society" program of social legislation: Job Corps, Medicare, Voting Rights Bill, aid to education.

▦ Appointed first black cabinet member, Robert Weaver, Department of Housing and Urban Development, and first black Supreme Court Justice, Thurgood Marshall.

▦ Retired at the end of 1968 term because of expansion of Viet Nam War.

AUGUST 28, 1963
March on Washington, D. C.

More than 200,000 Americans marched in Washington, D. C., and gathered in front of the Lincoln Memorial to tell the world that they wanted liberty, freedom, and justice for *all*. This date was one of the most significant in the history of the civil rights struggle in America. Among the leaders of the march was Reverend Dr. Martin Luther King, Jr., who addressed the crowd with his now historic speech that began with the words, "I have a dream . . ." and ended with:

> When we allow freedom to ring—when we let it ring from every village and from every hamlet, from every state and every city, we will be able to speed up that day when all of God's children, black men and white men, Jews and Gentiles, Protestants and Catholics, will be able to join hands and sing in the words of the old Negro spiritual: "Free at last, Free at last! Thank God almighty, we are free at least."

APPENDIX 1: Bibliography for Teacher Reference

GENERAL

The materials listed below, which are not discussed within the text, are reference materials that will further implement the celebration of important dates and events in elementary school classrooms.

Arbuthnot, May Hill, and Dorothy M. Broderick, comps. *Time for Biography* (Scott, Foresman, 1969).
Selections from popular biographies written for children of such people as United States presidents, explorers, scientists, heroes of American history, and communicators. Older students will be able to read most of the selections on their own.

Arbuthnot, May Hill, and Shelton L. Root, Jr., comps. *Time for Poetry* (Scott, Foresman, 1968).
The section, "Round the Calendar," features poetry about specific holidays, events, and the seasons.

Clemens, James R. *Creative Holidays: 100 Unusual Holiday Ideas* (Educational Insights, Inc., 1971).
A box of 4 x 6 inch cards giving many ideas for major holidays and important celebrations including crafts, projects, songs, and bulletin board displays.

Emrich, Duncan, comp. *The Hodgepodge Book: An Almanac of American Folklore* (Four Winds Press, 1972).
Everyone will have a hodgepodge of a time with this volume. "The Seasons of the Year," "The Months of the Year," and "Very Special Days of the Year" offer poetry, songs, sayings—all culled from Americana. Illustrated by Ib Ohlsson.

Hopkins, Lee Bennett. *Important Dates in Afro-American History* (Watts, 1969).

Although intended for upper-grade children, this volume can serve as a teacher reference. Illustrated with photographs, the book is a fully indexed day-to-day guide to people, places, and events relating to black America.

Jackdaws (Grossman Publishers).

Jackdaws, geared to upper-elementary grades, are durable packets of material filled with a bounty of goodies to bring important annual events, persons, or places dramatically to life. Each packet includes primary, hard-to-get materials in facsimile form—charts, posters, letters, maps, etc.—five to eight individual broadsheets describing major aspects of topics, and a guide for teachers. One example is *The American Revolution*, which features nine attractive items including a map of the fighting of Bunker Hill, a copy of the Declaration of Independence, and the June 3, 1783, edition of the South Carolina *Gazette*. Other topics include *The California Gold Rush: 1849, Young Shakespeare,* and *The Development of Writing*. Write for a descriptive catalog.

Krythe, Maymie R. *All About American Holidays* (Harper, 1962).

Discusses over fifty patriotic, religious, ethnic, and other holidays observed in the United States.

————. *All About the Months* (Harper, 1966).

Histories, discussions of birthstones and flowers, and quotations about each month make this an informative volume.

Larrick, Nancy, comp. *More Poetry for Holidays* (Garrard, 1973).

Since this anthology, and the one below, are for children, teachers will find them doubly useful. The poems are arranged in calendar order beginning with New Year's Day. An appendix, "Special Days Have Special Meanings," gives brief information on each of the holidays and events discussed in the book. Drawings by Harold Berson.

————. *Poetry for Holidays* (Garrard, 1966).

Features poems for Halloween, Thanksgiving, Christmas, New

[216]

Year's Day, St. Valentine's Day, St. Patrick's Day, Easter, May Day, Fourth of July, and birthdays. Illustrated by Kelly Oechsli.

Newmann, Dana. *The Teacher's Almanack* (Center for Applied Research, 1974).
Arranged from September through June, chapters give listings of important dates, helpful teaching hints, and ideas for bulletin board displays and arts and crafts projects.

Robbins, Ireene. *Elementary Teacher's Arts and Crafts Ideas for Every Month of the Year* (Parker, 1970).
Four hundred and fourteen projects are described to encourage children to express how they feel about holidays, special events, and the changing seasons. Arranged according to the calendar. Projects can be made with basic art supplies and materials found around the home. A treasury of ideas.

Sanders, Sandra. *Easy Ways with Holidays* (Scholastic Book Services, 1970, paper).
Word games, songs, contests, and projects are featured with "Facts for the Class" and special activities to tie in with celebrations that occur throughout the school year.

Sechrist, Elizabeth Hough, and Janette Woolsey. *New Plays for Red Letter Days* (Macrae Smith, 1953).
Twenty-five original plays for children in the upper grades are featured.

Sechrist, Elizabeth Hough. *Red Letter Days: A Book of Holiday Customs* (Macrae Smith, 1965, rev. ed.).
Although this book is intended for upper-grade students, teachers will find many interesting facts about special holidays of the year to share with all age groups. A chapter on the "Story of the Calendar" is included.

RESOURCES FOR TEACHING ABOUT THE
UNITED STATES PRESIDENTS

For All Ages

Lucky Chart of Presidents of the United States (Scholastic Book Services).

Engraved portraits of all the presidents including terms of office, significant events, major trends in country's growth. This chart is 58 x 20½ inches.

Portraits of the Presidents (Bowmar).

A high-quality set of 11 x 14 inch art prints on heavy art board with a nonglare plastic coating. Write to Bowmar for its illustrated materials on presidents.

For Upper Grades

Barclay, Barbara. *Lamps to Light the Way: Our Presidents* (Bowmar, 1970).

A handsome, excellent guide to biographies of the presidents and the achievements in their public careers. Illustrated with photographs, etchings, lithographs, and cartoons. A teacher's manual is also available.

Blassingame, Wyatt. *The Look-It-Up Book of Presidents* (Random House, 1968).

Biographies are accompanied by full-color illustrations.

Cary, Sturges. *Arrow Book of Presidents* (Scholastic Book Services, 1972, paper).

Fascinating facts about the presidents are given in an easy-to-read format.

Coy, Harold. *Presidents* (Watts, 1973, paper).

Brief, but fact-filled biographies presented with explanations of the presidency, including how it began, who can be president, inauguration day, and presidential duties. A photograph of each president is included.

Songs of the Presidency (Bowmar).

This 33⅓ LP recording presents a panorama of political songs with narrations that can be used quite effectively in upper-grade classrooms.

So You Want to Run for President (Scholastic Book Services).
A complete game on a giant poster to help create the drama of a presidential election.

APPENDIX 2: Sources of Educational Materials Cited

Abelard-Schuman, 257 Park Ave. South, New York, N.Y. 10010

Abingdon Press, 201 Eighth Ave. South, Nashville, Tenn. 37203

Association on American Indian Affairs, 432 Park Ave. South, New York, N.Y. 10016

Atheneum Publishers, 122 East 42nd St., New York, N.Y. 10017

Beacon Press, 25 Beacon St., Boston, Mass. 02108

Bowmar, Box 3623, Glendale, Calif. 91201

Broadside Press, 12651 Old Mill Pl., Detroit, Mich. 48238

Center for Applied Research, 521 Fifth Ave., New York, N.Y. 10017

Children's Press, 1224 W. Van Buren St., Chicago, Ill. 60607

Citation Press, 50 West 44th St., New York, N.Y. 10036

Coward, McCann & Geoghegan, 200 Madison Ave., New York, N.Y. 10016

Crowell (Thomas Y.) Co., 666 Fifth Ave., New York, N.Y. 10022

Delacorte Press, 1 Dag Hammarskjold Plaza, New York, N.Y. 10017

Dell Publishing Co., Inc., 1 Dag Hammarskjold Plaza, New York, N.Y. 10017

Dial Press, Inc., 1 Dag Hammarskjold Plaza, New York, N.Y. 10017

Dodd, Mead, 79 Madison Ave., New York, N.Y. 10016

Dorrance & Co., Inc., 1617 J. F. Kennedy Blvd., Philadelphia, Pa. 19103

Doubleday & Co., Inc., 277 Park Ave., New York, N.Y. 10017

Dutton (E. P.) & Co., Inc., 201 Park Ave. South, New York, N.Y. 10003

Educational Insights, Inc., 423 South Hindry Ave., Inglewood, Calif. 90301

Enrichment, Scholastic Audio-Visual, 906 Sylvan Ave., Englewood Cliffs, N.J. 07632

Farrar, Straus & Giroux, Inc., 19 Union Square West, New York, N.Y. 10003

Folkways Records, 43 West 61th St., New York, N.Y. 10023

Follett Publishing Co., 1010 West Washington Blvd., Chicago, Ill. 60607

Four Winds Press, 50 West 44th St., New York, N.Y. 10036

Gale Research, Book Tower, Detroit, Mich. 48226

Garrard Publishing Co., 1607 North Market St., Champaign, Ill. 61820

Giant Photos, Box 406, Rockford, Ill. 61105

Grossman Publishers, 625 Madison Ave., New York, N.Y. 10022

Harper & Row, Publishers, 10 East 53rd St., New York, N.Y. 10022

Harvey House, Inc., Irvington-on-Hudson, N.Y. 10533

Heath (D.C.) & Co., 125 Spring St., Lexington, Mass. 02173

Holt, Rinehart and Winston, 383 Madison Ave., New York, N.Y. 10017

Houghton Mifflin Co., 2 Park St., Boston, Mass. 02107

Hubbard Press, 2855 Shermer Rd., Northbrook, Ill. 60062

Instructor Publications, Dansville, N.Y. 14437

Knopf (Alfred A)., 201 East 50th St., New York, N.Y. 10022

Lippincott (J. B.), East Washington St., Philadelphia, Pa. 19105

Little, Brown & Co., 34 Beacon St., Boston, Mass. 02106

Macmillan Publishing Co., 866 Third Ave., New York, N.Y. 10022

Macrae Smith Co., 225 South 135th St., Philadelphia, Pa. 19102

McGraw-Hill Book Co., 1221 Ave. of the Americas, New York, N.Y. 10020

Miller-Brody Productions, Inc., 342 Madison Ave., New York, N.Y. 10017

Morrow (William S.) & Co., Inc., 105 Madison Ave., New York, N.Y. 10016

Nelson (Thomas) 407 Seventh Ave. South, Nashville, Tenn. 37203

New York Public Library, Fifth Ave. and 42nd St., New York, N.Y. 10036

Norton (W. W.) & Co., 55 Fifth Ave., New York, N.Y. 10003
Pantheon Books, 201 East 50th St., New York, N.Y. 10022
Parents' Magazine Press, 52 Vanderbilt Ave., New York, N.Y. 10017
Pocket Books, 1 West 39th St., New York, N.Y. 10018
Prentice-Hall, Inc., Englewood Cliffs, N.J. 07632
Putnam's (G. P.) Sons, 200 Madison Ave., New York, N.Y. 10016
Rand McNally & Co., Box 7600, Chicago, Ill. 60680
Random House, 201 East 50th St., New York, N.Y. 10022
Scholastic Audio-Visual, 906 Sylvan Ave., Englewood Cliffs, N.J. 07632
Scholastic Book Services, 50 West 44th St., New York, N.Y. 10036
Scott, Foresman, 1900 East Lake Ave., Glenview, Ill. 60025
Scribner's (Charles) Sons, 597 Fifth Ave., New York, N.Y. 10017
Seabury Press, 815 Second Ave., New York, N.Y. 10017
Simon & Schuster, 630 Fifth Ave., New York, N.Y. 10020
Spoken Arts, Inc. 310 North Ave., New Rochelle, N.Y. 10801
Time-Life Books, Time & Life Bldg., Rockefeller Center, New York, N.Y. 10020
University of Illinois Press, Urbana, Ill. 61801
Walck (Henry Z.), Inc., 19 Union Square West, New York, N.Y. 10003
Walker & Co., 720 Fifth Ave., New York, N.Y. 10019
Watts (Franklin), Inc., 730 Fifth Ave., New York, N.Y. 10019
Weston Woods, Weston, Conn. 06880
World Publishing Co., 110 East 59th St., New York, N.Y. 10022
Yale University Press, 302 Temple St., New Haven, Conn. 06511